StairStops

Using John Magee's Basing Points to Ratchet Stops in Trends

This may be the most important book on stops of this decade for the general investor.

Professor Henry Pruden, PhD.
Golden Gate University

W.H.C. Bassetti
Coauthor/Editor Edwards & Magee's
Technical Analysis of Stock Trends, 9th Edition

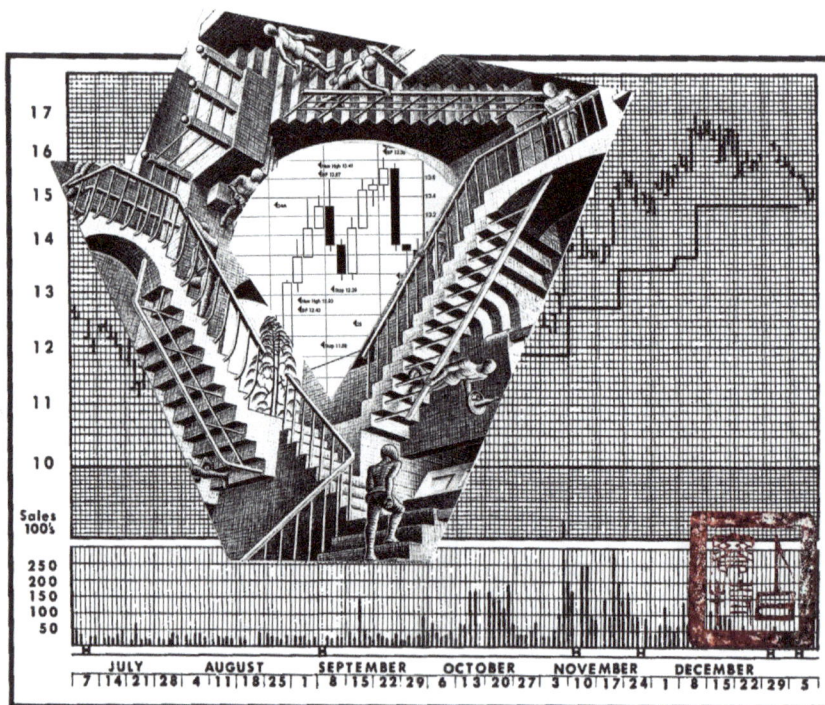

International Standard Book Number -13 978-0-9822-2190-7

———————————

Library of Congress Cataloging–in-Publication Data

Bassetti, W.H.C. (William Hart Charles, 1937)
  StairStops Using Basing Points to Ratchet Stops in Bull and Bear Markets/ W.H.C. Bassetti
  ISBN 978-0-9822-2190-7
1. Investment Analysis. 2. Stock Markets. 3. Stock Exchanges—United States. 4. Securities—United States. I Bassetti, W.H.C. II. Title

———————————

Visit the MaoMao Press Website at:
www.edwards-magee.com/maomaopress.html

Stair Stops

Stair Stops

Stair Stops

Stair Stops

Stair Stops

mission

Acknowledgements

For professional assistance: Jack Schannep, Robert W. Colby, Curtis Faith, Greg Morris and John Murphy, Tim Knight and Chi Huang.

For assistance at Taylor and Francis: Richard O'Hanley, Raymond O'Connell, Pat Roberson, Andrea Demby, and Roy Barnhill.

For research assistance and manuscript preparation: Brian Brooker and Grace Ryan, my fearsomely bright and efficient teaching and research assistants. And my inimitable technical assistants, Samuel W.D. Bassetti and Carlos Bassetti.

At Golden Gate University for ongoing support and assistance: Professor Henry Pruden, Barbara Karlin, Janice Carter, Tracy Weed and Cassandra Dilosa.

Special appreciation goes to makers of software packages and their supportive executives for software used in the preparation of this and previous books.

John Slauson
Adaptick
1082 East 8175 South
Sandy, UT 84094
www.adaptick.com

Steven Hill
AIQ Systems
P.O. Box 7530
Incline Village, NV 89452
702-831-2999
www.AIQsystems.com

Alan McNichol
Metastock
Equis International, Inc.
3950 S. 700 East, Suite 100
Salt Lake City, UT 84107
www.equis.com

Bill Cruz, Ralph Cruz, Darla Tuttle
Tradestation Omega Research
14257 SW 119th Avenue
Miami, FL 33186
305-485-7599
www.tradestation.com

Tim Knight, Chi Huang
Prophet Financial Systems, Inc.
658 High Street
Palo Alto, CA 94301
www.prophet.net
http://tradertim.blogspot.

Greg Morris, John Murphy
Stockcharts.com, Inc.
11241 Willows Road, #140
Redmond, WA 98052
www.stockcharts.com

Table of Contents

Table of Figures

Introduction

Tucked quietly away in the shell of Chapter 28 of Technical Analysis of Stock Trends is a trend following procedure that is the pearl of John Magee's work: The Basing Points Procedure.

As with Fermat's Last Theorem Magee left some anomalies in the Basing Points Procedure, but his work is sufficiently clear to summarize as follows:

In an orderly market (bull market assumed, bear market mirror image) prices ascend in waves. An up wave, then a down wave. Students of Dow Theory will immediately recognize Dow's observation. Sink a stake on the beach at the highest reach of a wave; then sink a new stake at the height of the next wave. So long as higher highs are achieved the tide is rising. When the highs begin to fall short of previous stakes the tide has turned and is running out.

In an uptrend the price rises, then recedes, making a higher low, then rises, making a higher high, then recedes, making a higher low, then rises – and the pattern comprises a bull trend: higher highs and higher lows.

Basing Points are wave lows upon which we base the calculation of stops.

Magee (among others) observed that "they" (or the market, or the specialists, or the market makers or ... whoever...) probe for stops during a down wave. So a stock (or commodity, or bond, or currency) rises to 10 and then falls to 5, rises to 11 and falls to 6 where market forces (whoever or whatever they are) will attempt to take out the low at 5.

Exacerbating volatility, or creating it in the first place, is not a new game. In Charles MacKay's classic, *Extraordinary Popular Delusions and the Madness of Crowds*, the trading of tulip bulbs replaced sober commerce and business as the occupation of Holland, and enormous fortunes were made trading the tubers. Blocks of real estate, breweries, assets of real and large value were traded for one tulip bulb. And MacKay produced my favorite paragraphs in the literature of finance:

"A golden bait hung temptingly out before the people, and one after the other, they rushed to the tulip-marts, like flies around a honey pot. Every one imagined that the passion for tulips would last forever, and that the wealthy from every part of the world would send to Holland, and pay whatever prices were asked for them."

"The demand for tulips of a rare species increased so much in the year 1636 that regular marts for their sale were established on the Stock Exchanges of Amsterdam, in Rotterdam, Harlaem, Leyden, Alkmar, Hoorn, and other towns. Symptoms of gambling now became, for the first time, apparent. *The stock jobbers, ever on the alert for a new speculation, dealt largely in tulips, making use of all the means they so well knew how to employ to cause fluctuations in prices.*" (Italics mine.)

Trading and Trending

In addition there are two (and only two, leaving out spreading and arbitrage) basic methodologies employed in the markets: Trend following and trading. Actually, trading is also trend following on short to very short time scales. After all a scalper who buys at 1/2 wants to sell at 3/4. In minutes. Or seconds. The trender wants to buy at 100 and sell at 150. In months, or years. The distinguishing difference between them is this, trend followers buy strength and sell weakness. Traders buy weakness and sell strength. This methodology in itself will exacerbate volatility.

Which is better? At this point I like to tell the story I tell my graduate students about John Kennedy, or perhaps it was Harry Truman, who remarked to a visitor that he was looking for a one armed economist. And why is that the visitor asked. Well it's because every time I talk to an economist he says on-the-one-hand this occurs, and on-the-other-hand that occurs.

So, on the one hand over time the trend follower wins biggest and best (see the record of the Dow Theory in the 9th edition of Technical Analysis of Stock Trends). On the other hand over the short time span the trader (if skilled) may see greater short term profits and less equity volatility. Considerably less skill is necessary to be a long term trend follower. Especially if Magee type methods are used.

Whether a trader or a trend follower, Magee's Basing Point Procedure is useful in trading and investing. It is also extremely useful as a theoretical appreciation of the nature of trends.

Editorial Practices

In the first edition of this book, I have often (but not always) indicated where new material will be inserted in the printed edition. In this way the reader can see where the book is going and can be enticed to proceed from buying the first edition to springing for the entire printed work.

Figures, or charts, are idiosyncratically numbered. A separate List of Figures contents is furnished. Since charts come from disparate sources I have created a figure number for this book. When I refer to a figure in the text this number is appended after the reference, thus, (Figure 210.1.1 (3)".

Chart prices may appear eccentric also. What is obviously the same chart will have different prices at different places in the text. This is because the chart picture was taken before (or after) a stock split. Clearly unimportant. The pattern is the important thing.

As was my practice with the 9th Edition of Technical Analysis of Stock Trends I have supplemented the text (ebook and full book) with material at the www. edwards-magee.com website. (www.edwards-magee. com/stairstops.html. So the reader can download PDFs of charts and supplementary material, enlarge it, and study details difficult to discriminate in this smaller format.

Organization of this Book

In order that Magee be allowed to speak for himself, and that the reader be allowed the benefit of his wide and deep experience, the first chapter is devoted to Magee's exposition of the method from Technical Analysis of Stock Trends. Chapter 2 is devoted to my effort, primarily from the 9th Edition, to clarify Magee's work and clear up some of the anomalies of his presentation. In the 9th Edition I clarified the setting of Basing Points set on wave lows. I believe that this is an inherently conservative way to use the method.

But there is another part of the procedure that is important and definitely worth use by the more skilled technician. That is, the setting of Basing Points according to the establishment of new highs as well as wave lows. I have called these two approaches Variant 1 and Variant 2. Variant 2 being the entire procedure. In Chapter 3 I lay out the entire Variant 2 procedure with instructions and illustrations. In Chapter 4 I address the question of filter calculation, citing both Magee's work on the subject and some pragmatic observations. In Chapter 5 the detailed day by day use of the procedure is illustrated. This step by step, day by day exposition should clear up confusion as to how the Basing Point is found. Chapter 6 shows how the method was used in real time to short the great bear market of 2008-2009. In the Appendix I offer the reader a drill, or exercise which will give some practice in using the method. Included here are blank charts which the reader may practice his marking of Basing Points. In my seminars I start with the drill rather than the exposition of the method. The surprises students experience are often enlightening...in many senses. The reader might want to consider reading the book back to front. That is, starting with the exercise and then turning to the front of the book. As an endpiece I reproduce a zen enso made for me by Tanahashi, the translator of Morihei Ueshiba's Aikido masterpiece, titled "What to think about while putting."

Chapter 1

Defining Wave Highs and Lows
(From Chapter 28 of Technical Analysis of Stock Trends)

chapter *twenty-eight*
What Is a Bottom — What Is a Top?

EN9: In this extremely important chapter I have left intact Magee's usage of "Tops and Bottoms". It will be less potentially confusing for the reader to think of "highs and lows" as that terminology is commonly used in the business in the modern era. Also, thinking in terms of highs and lows is an important concept in itself. Thus, for a bull trend, higher highs, higher lows. When this pattern is broken in an important way the trader should be alert for a trend change. And, as the use of eighths is of the essence in Figure 210, I have left the discussion in eighths while the reader knows that decimals are now used in the markets.

In this chapter, we are not talking about what makes a Major Top or Bottom, nor what makes an *Intermediate* Top or Bottom. We are speaking of the Minor Tops and Bottoms that give us important hooks on which to hang our technical operations. Stop-order levels, trendlines, objectives, Supports and Resistances are determined by these *Minor* Tops and Bottoms. They are of prime importance to us as traders.

Usually, these Minor Tops and Bottoms are well marked and perfectly clear. Often they are not. Sometimes, it is not possible to say definitely that this or that place is or is not a Top or Bottom. But it is possible to set certain

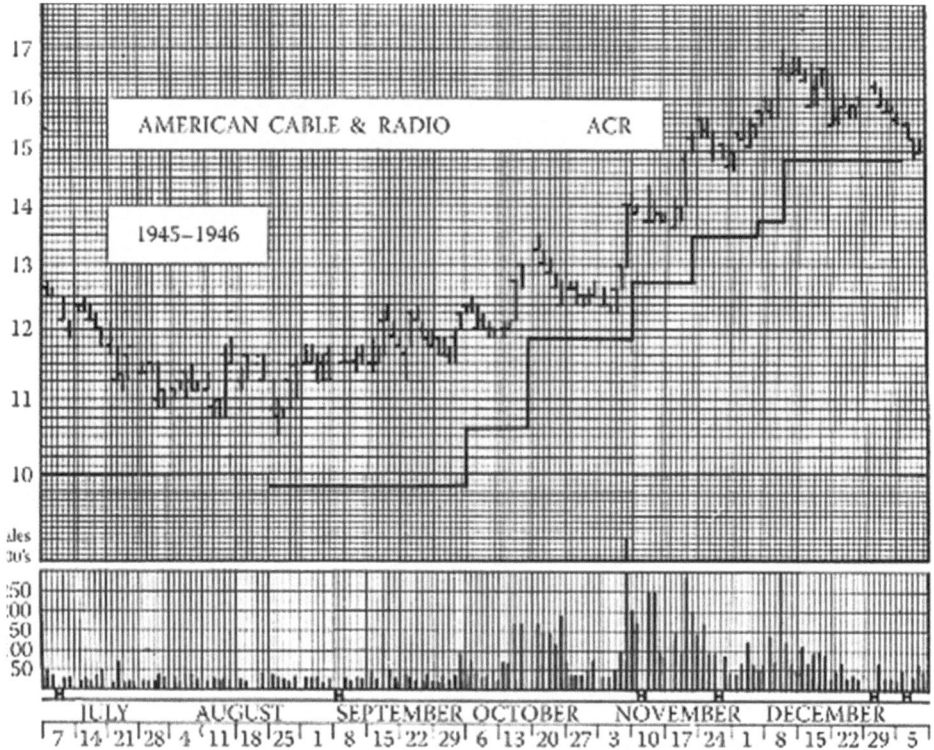

Figure 1. Figure 210 from Technical Analysis of Stock Trends

Figure 210: "Advance of a protective stop order in a long commitment. The daily chart of American Cable and Radio in the summer of 1945 made a Rounded Bottom, part of a long period of Consolidation following the advance which ended in July 1944. A breakout on heavy volume occurred September 12, and purchases were then possible on any Minor Reactions.

standards, practical working rules, that will help us in making these points; and these rules will not fail us too often.

A good rule for setting stop levels is to consider that a Bottom has been made when the stock has moved "three days away" from the day marking the suspected low of the Bottom. If a stock reacts for some days and finally makes a low at 24, with a high for that day at 25, then we will not have an established Bottom until we have had *3 days* in which the stock sells at no lower than 25 1/8. The entire price range for 3 full days must be entirely above the top price for the day making the low. This is the "three days away" rule, and it would apply in reverse in declining markets, where the range for 3 days must be entirely below the entire range of the day making the high.

This gives a rule for setting an original stop order. It also gives a rule for changing the stop order. As soon as the stock has moved 3 days away from a new Bottom, we move the stop order to a position below that Bottom. (We have already explained in Chapter 27 how we determine the distance this stop level should be below the Bottom.)

The first protective stop would immediately be placed 6% below the previous Minor Bottom of August 21, using the table given in Chapter 27. This would put the stop level at 9 7/8. On September 19 and 20, we would have 2 days of market action entirely "away" from the September 17 Minor Bottom, and, on September 28, a third day. We would then move the stop up to 6% under the September 17 Bottom, or to 10 5/8. The next move would come after the new high closing of October 11, which is more than 3% higher than the October 1 Minor Peak. The stop would now be placed at 11 7/8. On November 2, a new high close was registered more than 3% over the October 15 Minor Peak; the stop would be raised to 12 3/4. On November 15, another high closing topped by over 3% the Minor Peak made on November

7. The stop would be moved up again, this time to 13 1/2. November 29 made the third day the entire range was "three days away" from the November 26 Bottom, and the stop was upped to 13 3/4. The closing on December 5 gave us a 3% advance over the November 17 high, and again we moved the stop, raising it to 14 7/8. Finally, on January 3, 1946, this stop was caught as shown on the chart. In a Bear Market, protective stops would be moved down in exactly the same manner to protect a short sale. *EN9: A number of inconsistencies exist in this figure and caption which are clarified later in the text.*"

Protective stops for long stocks can move only up. A stop level, once established, is never to be moved down except when the stock goes ex-dividend or ex-rights; then the stop may be dropped the amount of the dividend or rights. Similarly, protective stops for short sales are to be moved only down, and may not be raised. (In the case of ex-dividends and ex-rights, the short-sale stop would be dropped the amount of the dividend or rights.)

There are certain situations where it is difficult to determine Bottoms and Tops; where, indeed, it seems as though a Consolidation or Correction had been made without any significant move in the Secondary Direction. In such cases (as contrasted to the obvious situation where the stock moves up or down in series of well-marked steps and reactions, like a staircase), you will need all your judgment and experience to determine where the Minor Basing Points actually occur.

Basing Points

Let us call the levels which determine where stops should be placed Basing Points. In a Bull Market Move, we will consider the Bottom of each Minor Reaction as a Basing Point, from which we will figure our stop-order level as soon as the stock has moved up to "three days away." We will also use each Minor Top as a Basing Point in a Bull Move. In a Bear Market, we will consider the Tops of each rally and also each Minor Bottom as Basing Points for the protective stops, in the same way.

Where a stock makes a substantial move in the Primary Direction, say a move of 15% or more, and then moves back at least 40% of the distance covered from the previous Basing Point to the end of the Primary Move, that surely gives us a Basing Point as soon as the stock again starts off in the Primary Direction. However, if the stock reacts less than 40%, perhaps even marks time at the same level for a week or more, that should also be considered a Basing Point as soon as the move in the Primary Direction is continued (provided the volume indications are right).

The daily volume, as we have seen, is like the trained nurse's clinical thermometer; it tells a great deal about what is happening in a stock, more than the superficial symptoms of price alone. There are three times at which you may look for exceptionally heavy volume: (1) on the day of breakout from a pattern or a period of inaction, especially if the breakout is on the upside; (2) on the day on which the stock goes into new ground in the Primary or Intermediate Direction, that is, goes above the last Minor Top in a Bull Market, or below the last Minor Bottom in a Bear Market; and (3) the day on which the Minor Move is completed or nearly completed, that is, the new Minor Top in a Bull Market and the Minor Bottom in a Bear Market. To this we might add that extra heavy volume on any other day during a move in the Primary Direction is likely to indicate that the move is at an end and will not complete the hoped-for advance or decline.

Now, after a Minor Top has occurred, the stock now being in new high ground, and the Top having been made on very heavy volume, we may look for the corrective move. Ordinarily, that would be a decline of several days, a week, sometimes longer. Occasionally, the correction, as we said a few paragraphs back, will take the form of a horizontal hesitation lasting a week or more without any particular corrective move in the downward direction. Where there is a downward correction, it is likely to come down to or near the Top of the last previous Minor High (support). Also, and often at the same time, the corrective move will carry down to the Basic Trendline drawn through two or more previous Minor Bottoms; or to the "parallel"; or to a trendline drawn through the last two or more previous Minor Tops. If the corrective move is horizontal, it is likely to run out until it meets one of these lines.

In any case, the thing to watch for is the decline of volume. If the trading shrinks, perhaps irregularly, but on the whole, steadily, for some days after a new Top has been made, during which time the stock either reacts or, at any rate, makes no progress in the Primary Direction, then you are justified in considering this as a Minor Correction. If the stock now continues the Primary Move and gets to a point that is "three-days-away," you can consider the Bottom (that is, the point you draw your trendline through, not necessarily the extreme low point in the case of horizontal moves) as a new Basing Point.

Where a stock is starting what appears to be a new move, a breakout from a period of vacillating moves, it is sometimes hard to say precisely what point should be considered the Bottom. There may be several small and indecisive moves on low volume preceding the real breakout. In such a case, we would consider the appearance of high volume as the breakout signal, and set our Basing Point at the low point immediately preceding this signal. There will usually be such a point on one of the low-volume days in the 3 or 4 days just before the breakout.

All that has been said about Basing Points in a Bull Market would also be true, in reverse, in a Bear Market, except that heavy volume does not always accompany a downside breakout.

Now there comes the difficult and distressing situation where the stock, having made a long runaway move (let us assume it is an upward move), starts out, apparently, to make a Flag, and is bought after a sufficient correction of 40% with a decline of volume, and then continues to go down steadily, without any rallies and without any clear volume indications. This is an unusual situation, but it does happen on both the upside and the downside, from time to time. In the case we have just mentioned, we would look for Support Levels (Consolidation Patterns, Multiple Tops, etc.) formed on the way down in the previous trend, and lying below the level at which we purchased the stock. We would use these supports as Basing Points rather than hold a stop under the extreme Bottom of the vertical move.

In many cases of this type, you will not be able to find adequate Basing Points. Therefore, it seems unwise to try to get in on corrections after long runaway moves except: (1) where the stock has risen well above good Support that can serve as a Basing Point, or (2) where the stock is completely above all prices for several years and is moving "in the clear." (The reverse, of course: in Bear Markets, the stock should have fallen below a strong Resistance Area, or must be in new low ground for the past several months before you consider a short sale.) And in any case of this sort where you are thinking of a trade in a stock that appears to be making a Consolidation after a fast, long, vertical move, you must have pronounced and conspicuous drying up of volume throughout the formation of the Flag or Pennant Correction.

There is one more word of caution needed here regarding trading in an Intermediate Trend. A series of moves in a trend will often take place in very regular form. There may be a good trendline, and the reactions may be about 40% to 50% and may come back to the previous Minor Tops. The volume on the Corrections may shrink, with increasing volume on the new Tops. It is easy to start trading on such a "staircase" in the expectation that the moves will continue to be regular and consistent. But trends do not go on forever. Any Minor Top may be the last. The importance of finding your Basing Points is to enable you to get out, at best, on any closing violation of one of these points, and at worst, on your protective stop order. The volume may again come to your aid in this question of when to stop trading on a trend. Although you look for high volume on the Tops, you will be exceedingly suspicious of volume that is much higher than that on any of the preceding Minor Tops (or Bottoms in a Bear Market). The final, or the next-to-final, "blow-off" of a trend will usually show more volume than any of the Minor blow-offs along the way; and when you see such climactic volume, you should prepare to retire into your shell and wait for a full Correction of the entire series of moves making up your Intermediate Trend. Later, weeks later, or perhaps months later, you may find the stock has corrected 40% or more of the whole Intermediate Move and is resting quietly with very little activity. Then is the time to watch it for new opportunities and a new trend in the Primary Direction.

Editor's Note: In a book composed of nothing but important chapters this Chapter 28 might not get the emphasis it deserves from the unwary reader. In fact the procedure outlined here is of absolutely basic importance in analyzing and trading trends. So I have added to it material in Chapter 28.1 which has been of great importance to my trading and to the trading of my students.

Chapter 2

A Case Study of the Basing Points Procedure
(From Chapter 28.1 of Technical Analysis of Stock Trends)

chapter *twenty-eight.one*
Basing Points – Further Thoughts and Examples

The longer one thinks about the chart so casually tossed off in Figure 210 (fig. 1) the more he realizes that it embodies a profound and natural understanding of trends and the market.   Consider—wave up, wave recedes; wave up, wave recedes, and so on. As long as the trader or investor is not chased from his position by the corrective wave he will under normal circumstances ride the trend to its natural end. But locals and hedge funds and those who profit from volatility know that the previous low is where investors and traders set their stops. So in the ordinary flow of trading if they see an opportunity to take out an important low they will do it. If possible. And it is sometimes possible. And the low sometimes falls from the natural flow of trading.

Bruce Kovner, on being interviewed by Jack Schwager (Market Wizards), was asked where he set his stops. "Where they're hard to get to," he said. A stop set on a Basing Point with a prudently calculated filter is hard to get to, unless the market has truly reversed direction. In fact, what is a long term moving average but a lagging stop with a filter built in?

And what are Basing Points but the marking of highs and lows in full realization that a pattern of higher highs and higher lows is a bull trend, and when that pattern changes to one of lower highs and lower lows the trend is changing, or has changed. This is the principle behind Dow Theory, and it is the principle behind trading trends of lesser duration than Dow trends. And, as is quickly realized, a pattern of lower highs and lower lows means inevitably that the trend line has been broken.

As for Figure 210 (fig. 1), Mark Twain had some cogent comments on it. He said that anyone trying to make sense of it would go crazy, and anyone trying to justify the prices with the chart would be shot. Figure 210 preserves unexplainable conundrums and conflicts carefully preserved since the earliest editions. The reader is urged to take it as a concept rather than using it as a lesson. Therefore let me codify the rules implicitly presented in the Figure:

1. A high is made, being recognized by no higher prices occurring for the moment.

2. Prices recede and a low is made. This low is found by watching each day after the previous high until no lower prices are

made. As prices begin to rise again we note each day on which prices are completely out of the range of our low day candidate.

3.   When three such days are observed before a new high is made we mark the candidate day as a Basing Point and raise our stop to 6% (or x%) under the low of the Basing Point day.

4.   If a new high is made after a high before a three days away Basing Point is made the process starts over from the new high.

5.   If the new high is 3% (or x%) higher than the previous high a new Basing Point is found at the low of the new high day.

The Basing Points Paradigm

By no means will every issue be amenable to this kind of analysis. But the method is so paradigmatic that it is worth examining at greater length. And like virtually every other method of classical chart analysis it must be used with caution and good and thoughtful judgment. Sometimes on some stocks it will seem to work as smooth as silicon lubricant and on other issues it will appear to be useless. However, even on recalcitrant issues the principles underlying the method will be of use, if not the actual method itself. With this in mind Figure 210.1 (fig. 2) is presented. The careful reader will see that the chart in this example uses only bottoms or lows in stop setting and does not advance stops on the making of new highs as in Figure 210 (fig. 1). This is done for instructional purposes and to keep the example simple for the general investor. More advanced traders will want to study and perhaps utilize the techniques in Figure 210.1.1 (fig. 4).

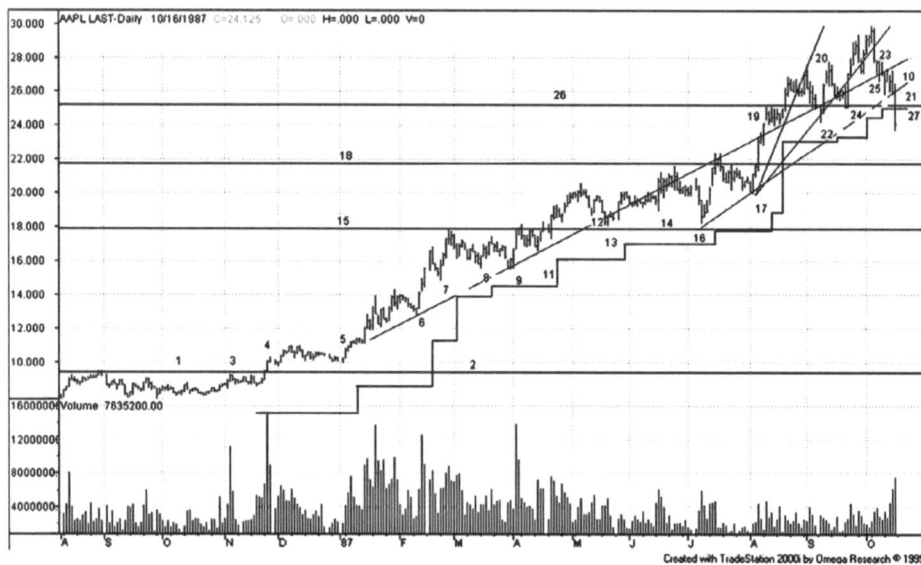

Figure 2. Figure 210.1 Apple Computer, Bull Market and 1987 Crash.
A near perfect example of the use of Basing Points for trading of a reasonably regular and smooth bull market.

Figure 210.1 (fig. 2) actually serves more than one instructional purpose. It illustrates a picture perfect case of the use of Basing Points, and it also illustrates a complete analysis of a bull market from entry to exit with keys marking events in the life of the market. Thus, the observation of Basing Points, the setting of the stops, the tracking of potentially false turns are all noted. The chart is accompanied by the keys. Originally the marked and keyed chart was used in graduate seminars at Golden Gate University for instructional purposes. Shortly it became obvious that marking the chart in this manner was extremely useful in trading. So it is suggested to the reader as a way of making his charts more communicative and more useful.

Key To Figure 210.1 Analysis

1. A rounding bottom, or perhaps a scallop
2. Resistance or breakout line
3. Wake up call on volume
4. Run Day, big volume; Breakout through line 2; Sure entry signal
5. First Basing Point (BP) Notice prior volume fall off in consolidation, and surge on run-day
6. BP
7. A weak BP (because of shallow retracement)
8. BP
9. Test of BP at 8
10. A trendline drawn after point 9
11. BP
12. BP candidate which fails 3 day rule
13. BP
14. A potential BP but not a very good one because new high has not been made from 13
15. A support/resistance line
16. BP
17. BP
18. A resistance/support line.
19. Flag which becomes BP
20. Trendline, but too steep to last.
21. Trendline.
22. BP
23. Trendline
24. BP
25. BP
26. Horizontal trend line – support
27. BP at 25 26.75 (stop 25.15) stopped out at 25.15

A Narrative of the Events in the Chart

1,2,3   Had we been asleep the event at number 3 should have awakened us. A volume day like this should catch the attention, and we begin paying attention to the stock and note the pattern that has been developing—the rounding bottom, or scallop.

4.   And at number 4 we see a 'run day' on heavy volume. A good signal for entry with the breaking of the horizontal line at 2. When we enter we set our stop 6% under the recent low. After entering on strength there is every possibility that some profit taking will occur as well as probing by locals to chase out arrivistes.

5.   We watch with interest for the first reaction. Each day we observe as a candidate for a possible 'Basing Point'. This occurs at 5 and we now begin to count 'days away' from the Basing Point, that is, days whose range is entirely outside the range of the candidate day, and which occur before a lower low is made. When the Basing Point at 5 is confirmed we raise our stop to 6% under 5.

6.   A higher high is made after 5 with a subsequent reaction to 6, which proves to be another Basing Point. So we raise our stop to 6% under 6.

7.   Prices continue to climb and another Basing Point is made at 7. The procedure is becoming clear: Find a Basing Point and establish a stop a prudent distance under it. If a new Basing Point is made raise the

stop. Watch with interest the reactions against the trend. Either they allow you to establish a new higher Basing Point, or they end your trade.

8,9   We find a new Basing Point at 8, raise our stop and draw the trendline at 10. At 9 we have a lower low than 8, but our 'filter', our 6% padding keeps our position intact. We do not lower our stops using 9 as a new Basing Point. One of the inviolable rules is that stops are never lowered. The filter is important, since traders try to take out nearby lows and exacerbate volatility. It is called the running of the sheep.

11.   At 11 we find a new, if tenuous Basing Point. An advance with a thin higher high.

12.   At 12 we have a candidate for a Basing Point which fails the 3 day rule.

13.   At 13 we find the Basing Point that is good and raise our stop.

14.   And at 14 we are confronted with a marginal situation. It is potential Basing Point. But a marginal one because a higher high was not made after 13.

15.   At 15 we are able to draw a line defining resistance—a line which will become a support line.

16.   At 16 we get a new Basing Point.

17.   At 17 we find a new Basing Point and at 18 we can identify a resistance line. The spurt across this line is both gratifying and a warning. Because it becomes a flagpole from which the flag at 19 flies. Flags and

flagpoles are messages that the market has heated up and now wants close watching. A flag can serve as a Basing Point, so we move our stop again, fully aware that the end may be approaching. The trendline at 20 is further confirmation of this environment due to its steepness. But we see two good anchor points in 16 and 17 and draw trendline 21—a better line to defend.

22. A good reaction finally occurs at 22 giving a strong Basing Point and good rationale for raising the stop. Notice the interesting fact that points 22 and 24 have come back to rest on the trendline we drew at 10. As the tempo has increased, and the volatility, 24 furnishes us another valid Basing Point.

24. As the tempo has increased and the volatility 24 furnishes us another valid Basing Point.

25. Even 25 is a valid point and we can now see the clear support line at 26.

27. When this line is pierced at 27 upon extraordinary volume, and in the process takes out our Basing Point stop from 25, it is clearly time to exit the train.

The Basing Point concept is even more thoroughly explored on the John Magee Technical Analysis website: www.edwards-magee.com. Materials will be found there which aid in the study of the method.

Chapter 3

The Complete Basing Points Procedure
Taking Into Consideration the Setting of Basing Points On Both Wave Lows and New Highs

As previously discussed by Magee the Basing Points Procedure may set Basing Points on both wave lows and on new highs. We find the wave low Basing Point by the three-days-away rule; we find the new high Basing Point by marking wave highs and subsequent new highs. So that when price exceeds by 3% the old wave high, or recent high, whether or not an intervening wave low has occurred, we may set the new Basing Point at the low of the new high day. If a new high were made subsequent to this new high we would reset the Basing Point again if we were using this variant of the procedure. I call it Variant 2.

Once again the one armed economist rules. On the one hand

raising the stops like this on new highs may easily result in being ejected from the position by a price dip; then you watch the train leaving the station on the way to incredible new highs amid much teeth gnashing and irritation. (Incidentally, if emotional distress occurs in this or other like situations it is a message to you that you are too emotionally attached to the market. Complete market maturity is not achieved until such situations can be viewed with relative equanimity. So that the event is viewed with detached interest and a plan to set things right.)

On the other hand after having accumulated large paper profits the issue collapses and snatches back from you a third (or more) of your hard earned profits. (If you had only advanced stops based on new highs!) Remember. The problem with Dow Theory (and trend following) is that you give up the first third of the move and the last third of the move and sometimes there isn't a middle third. As conventional market wisdom has it.

What essentially occurs when using Variant 2 of the procedure is: when blowoff or runaway conditions occur the procedure changes from selling weakness to selling strength. I believe very strongly in the variation of tactics generally. And I also am intimately familiar with the pitfalls of varying tactics. But I like the procedure in general and also think that knowing when to use it and when not can require a great deal of experience and emotional coolness in potentially high stress conditions.

If the entire (Variant 2) procedure is executed and also combined with a scale-in/scale-out plan the user may succeed in shooting the moon.

The phlegmatic Marc Antony (who sleeps well of night and is sleek and well fed) follows the conservative wave low method (Variant 1) and probably wins in the long run. The Variant 1 procedure is simpler and naturally expands to accommodate the high volatility market which ejects the trader attempting to escape the inevitable collapse; before going on to new completely unexpected heights.

So damned if you do, damned if you don't unless you are charmed, or kissed by the market fairy. Or lucky.

The Complete Basing Points Procedure

1.	A wave high is made, recognized by no higher prices coming for the moment. If this high is 3% (Magee's number, but could be a parameter) higher than the previous wave high (or the recent high in a run or blow-off) the Basing Point is raised to the low of the new high day. Obviously this comes into effect for the next trading day.

2.	Prices recede and a low is made. This low is found by watching each day after the previous high until no lower prices are made (a potential wave low, or Basing Point Candidate). As prices begin to rise again we note each day on which prices are completely out of the range of (away from) our low day candidate, or, a "day away."

3.	When three such days are observed (three-days-away) before a new low is made we mark the candidate day as a Basing Point and raise our stop to 6% (or x% since this is a parameter) under the low of the Basing Point day. Obviously the new stop is established the day after the three-days-away have occurred.

4.	If a new high is made without an intervening wave low Basing Point the

Two Charts Giving Long View Perspective on the Complete (Variant 2) Procedure

Figure 3. Chart: Figure 210.1.1   (The Missing Figure 210.1.1 from Technical Analysis of Stock Trends, 9th Edition)

This chart is a candlestick version of Figure 210.1. It illustrates the complete procedure, showing establishment of Basing Points made by wave lows and by higher highs. This is a blow up of the period in the chart where higher high conditions exist. As might be obvious the higher high rules begin to come into play late in the life of a trend, in runaway and blow-off stages. This is an overall view of the stages shown in the detail charts in Chapter 5.

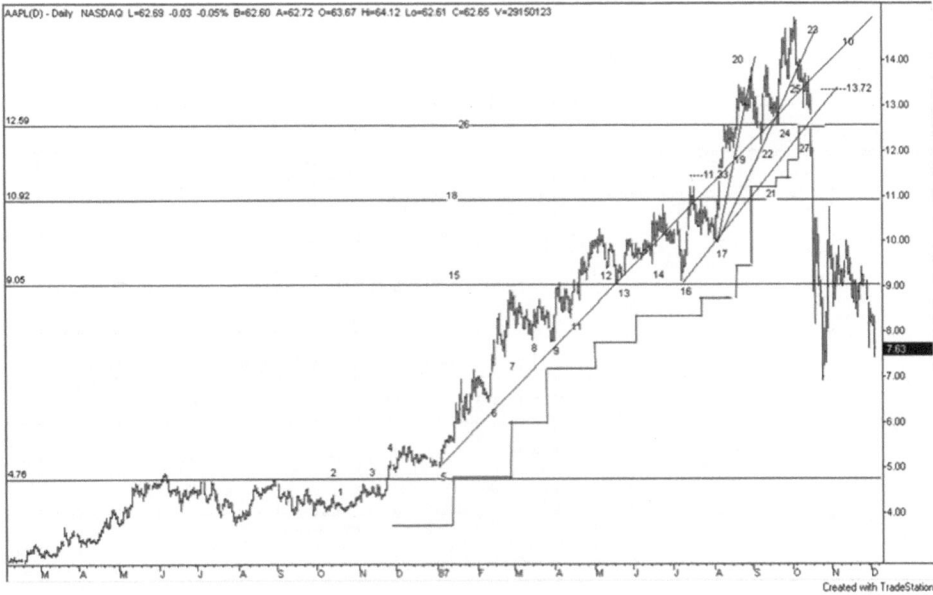

Figure 4. Chart: Figure 210.1.1 (Version 2)

This chart shows the trend from beginning to end as in Figure 210.1, with the addition of dotted lines to show where stops fell when computed from higher highs. The previous candlestick chart is used for the close-up analysis. This chart puts into broad perspective the relative level of stops using the Variant 2 method. As can be seen setting stops from new higher highs results in stops closer to the market prices. This can be good or bad, depending on what the market does to you.

There is another method Magee advocated for surging and blow off markets. He called this alternative method progressive stops. It is explained in the 9th edition. Strictly speaking while there is a variation in tactics involved in using new highs for stop calculation, this method is a twist on selling on strength. Variant 2 is still lagging stops behind prices. A pure strength selling method would attempt to time exit on a blow off day, or a key reversal day or a one day reversal, or even on a strong long running day up. This is perhaps a little easier to visualize on the downside. A panic selling day (which tends to finish at the lows) would provoke an exit on the close. Larger versions of these charts are at edwards-magee.com/stairstops.html.

process starts over from the new high.

5. If the new high is 3% (or x%) higher than the previous high (whether made from a wave low or wave high), or from surging prices continually making new highs, a new Basing Point is found at the low of the new high day. Thus, a price move which went from 10 to 10.3 to 10.61 to 10.93 would create new Basing Points at the low of each new high day.

The Representative Case Fully Analyzed
using wave lows and new highs

The case will not be unfamiliar to readers, and its use will fully highlight the differences found in the procedure. The same materials will be used, and the differences will be boldfaced in the text.

1. A rounding bottom, or perhaps a scallop
2. Resistance or breakout line
3. Wake up call on volume
4. Run Day, big volume; Breakout through line 2; sure entry signal
5. First Basing Point (BP) Notice prior volume fall off in consolidation, and surge on run-day
6. BP
7. A weak BP (because of shallow retracement)
8. BP
9. Test of BP at 8
10. A trendline drawn after point 9
11. BP
12. BP candidate which fails 3 day rule
13. BP
14. A potential BP but not a very good one because new high has not been made from 13
15. A support/resistance line
16. BP
16A. New High: 10.35
17. BP
17A. **New Higher High 10.81 Low BP 9.89 (+3% 11.13) Stop 9.30**
17B. **New Higher High 11.16 Low BP 10.58 (+3% 11.49) Stop 10.49**
17C. **New Higher High 11.62 Low BP 11.22 (+3% 11.96) Stop 10.55**
18. A resistance/support line
19. Flag which becomes BP. High 11.62
19A. **New Higher High 12.55 Low BP 11.91 (+3% 12.93) Stop 11.19**
20. Trendline, but too steep to last

21.   Trendline
22.   BP
23.   Trendline
24.   BP
24A. New Higher High 12.93 Low BP 12.43 (+3% 13.34) Stop 11.68
24B. New Higher High 13.41 Low BP 13.07 (+3% 13.81) Stop 12.29
25.   BP
25A. New Higher High 13.82 Low BP 13.36 (+3% 14.23) Stop 12.56
25B. Stopped out at 12.56
26.   Horizontal trend line
27.   BP at 25 (stop 11.80) Stopped out at 11.80

A Narrative of the events in the Chart

1,2,3   Had we been asleep the event at number 3 should have awakened us. A volume day like this should catch the attention, and we begin paying attention to the stock and note the pattern that has been developing—the rounding bottom, or scallop.

4.   And at number 4 we see a 'run day' on heavy volume. A good signal for entry with the breaking of the horizontal line at 2. When we enter we set our stop 6% under the recent low. After entering on strength there is every possibility that some profit taking will occur as well as probing by locals to chase out arrivistes.

5.   We watch with interest for the first reaction. Each day we observe as a candidate for a possible 'Basing Point'. This occurs at 5 and we now begin to count 'days away' from the Basing Point, that is, days whose range is entirely outside the range of the candidate day, and which occur before a lower low is made. When the Basing Point at 5 is confirmed we raise our stop to 6% under 5.

6.   A higher high is made after 5 with a subsequent reaction to 6, which proves to be another Basing Point. So we raise our stop to 6% under 6.

7.   Prices continue to climb and another Basing Point is made at 7. The procedure is becoming clear: Find a Basing Point and establish a stop a prudent distance under it. If a new Basing Point is made raise the stop. Watch with interest the reactions against the trend. Either they allow you

to establish a new higher Basing Point, or they end your trade.

8,9   We find a new Basing Point at 8, raise our stop and draw the trendline at 10. At 9 we have a lower low than 8, but our 'filter', our 6% padding keeps our position intact. We do not lower our stops using 9 as a new Basing Point. One of the inviolable rules is that stops are never lowered. The filter is important, since traders try to take out nearby lows and exacerbate volatility. It is called the running of the lambs.

11.   At 11 we find a new, if tenuous Basing Point. An advance with a thin higher high.

12.   At 12 we have a candidate for a Basing Point which fails the 3 day rule.

13.   At 13 we find the Basing Point that is good and raise our stop.

14.   And at 14 we are confronted with a marginal situation. It is potential Basing Point. But a marginal one because a higher high was not made after 13.

15.   At 15 we are able to draw a line defining resistance—a line which will become a support line.

16.   At 16 we get a Basing Point.

16A. New High: 10.35 (a benchmark)

17.   At 17 we find a new Basing Point and at 18 we can identify a resistance line. The spurt across this line is both gratifying and a warning. Because it becomes a flagpole

from which the flag at 19 flies. Flags and flagpoles are messages that the market has heated up and now wants close watching. A flag can serve as a Basing Point, so we move our stop again, fully aware that the end may be approaching. The trendline at 20 is further confirmation of this environment due to its steepness. But we see two good trendline anchor points in 16 and 17 and draw trendline 21—a better line to defend.

17A.   New Higher High 10.81 Low BP 9.89 (+3% 11.13)

17B.   New Higher High 11.16 Low BP 10.58 (+3% 11.49)

17C.   New Higher High 11.62 Low BP 11.22 (+3% 11.96)

19.   Flag which becomes BP. High 11.62

19A.   New Higher High 12.55 Low BP 11.91 (+3% 12.93) Stop 11.19

22.   A good reaction finally occurs at 22 giving a strong Basing Point and good rationale for raising the stop. Notice the interesting fact that points 22 and 24 have come back to rest on the trendline we drew at 10. As the tempo has increased, and the volatility, 24 furnishes us another valid Basing Point.

24A.   New Higher High 12.93 Low BP 12.43 (+3% 13.34) Stop 11.68

24B.   New Higher High 13.41 Low BP 13.07 (+3% 13.81) Stop 12.29

25. Even 25 is a valid point and we can now see the clear support line at 26.

25A. New Higher High 13.82 Low BP 13.36 (+3% 14.23) Stop 12.56

25B. Stopped out at 12.56

27. When this line is pierced at 12.56 upon extraordinary volume, and in the process takes out our Basing Point stop from 25, it is clearly time to exit the train.

Chapter 4

Calculating Filters, or Stop Distance, from Basing Point

In Chapter 27 of the 9th Edition Magee proposed a method for determining the size of the filter to be used in setting stops calculated from Basing Points. The table he used depended on the Sensitivity Index Appendix he had laboriously compiled from hand made charts. The Sensitivity Index might be looked on as a highly pragmatic form of beta, or as a hybrid of beta and volatility. In the modern context it needs refining, or substitution. I proposed, in the 8th Edition, that an alternate method could be used based on implied volatility.

It is important to remember, not just in this discussion, but in all discussions, that the general state of the market affects individual stock behavior. In a roaring general bull market (such as Microsoft in the 90s) a Basing Point may never be severely tested in an individual instrument. In a sideways mule market Basing Points may be frequently tested in the uptrend of an individual instrument. And in some stocks testing may occur as a regular phenomenon. The essential problem in calculating filters is obvious. A stop immediately under a low, or near a horizontal support line is a sitting duck. As the market searches for price equilibrium it probes down to find demand. We may look at this from two angles. One, it does this to suck in short sellers and to encourage weak holders to sell. Two, it does this to discover market-determined consensus price.

Either way as it hovers on price wave lows market mischief makers will attempt to take out the low and find stops placed too close. Depending on the general market trend this may be difficult, as in the Microsoft case or easy as in futures and volatile instruments. So the filter must be calibrated to the individual conditions of the market and the instrument.

A Pragmatic and Empirical Way to Determine Filter Size

The best and most naturalistic way of determining filter size is to analyze the issue at hand. Examine its volatility (not just its standard deviation, but also its average true range) its wave patterns and its characteristic habits. Included in this study should be special attention paid to behavior in three sigma conditions, or in abnormal market conditions. From this study will emerge the most appropriate filter size.

Alternatively we might do it by a table look up. If we were going to be punctilious in our filter calculation we would probably have a number of tables. We would want to know the rate of change of the market, and of the sector and of the instrument, and the volatilities of

Table of Stop Distances (Expressed in Percent of the Price of the Stock)			
Price	Conservative sensitivity under 0.75	Median sensitivity 0.75 to 1.25	Speculative sensitivity over 1.25
	Volatility under 0.40	Volatility 0.41–0.79	Volatility over 0.79
Over 100	5%	5%	5%
40 to 100	5%	5%	6%
20 to 40	5%	5%	8%
10 to 20	5%	6%	10%
5 to 10	7%	12%	
Under 5	5%	10%	15%
[a] Note: Ordinarily, stocks in these price ranges would not be in the conservative group.			

Figure 5. Table of Stop Distances from Technical Analysis of Stock Trends

these, and the beta, and we could go on and on until we had spent so much time that the market had closed and we had missed the trade.

So, for the creatively lazy (please include the author in this group) I include here a handmade quasi-scientific table for quick use. Traders are warned to examine this skeptically and validate it for their situations before backing it with money.

Here is Magee's table for comparison, (Figure 5) with my recommendations from the 8th Edition of Technical Analysis of Stock Trends. (Emmended for the current StairStops book.)

Filter (stop distance) Calculation

I am including here the table of Stop Distances from Chapter twenty-seven: Stop Orders, from the ninth edition:

Begin quote:
In any case, the stop distance, expressed as a percentage, is obtained by dividing the Normal Range-for-Price by 15.5, then multiplying by the Sensitivity Index, and multiplying this result by 5%. (This operation can be done most easily and quickly with a calculator or computer routine.)

All of the foregoing may seem needlessly complicated to the average reader. We realize that many will not care to take the time and trouble to work out an exact, scientific stop level for each of their occasional commitments. However, the method of determining where stops should be placed in a systematic and consistent way has been given in some detail here, so that the principles involved will be perfectly clear, and so that you can change or adapt the various factors if you feel your experience justifies changes.

For most ordinary purposes, a simplified table of stop distances will be sufficient. This table, which follows, gives you the approximate stop distance you would get by the method outlined above, for stocks in various price classifications and of various degrees of sensitivity.

Editor's Note: The informed reader may consider an alternative to Magee's Sensitivity Index which I have conjectured here — that is, basing the stop distance on volatility, which would present a dynamic method of adjustment. Implied volatility could also be used at the same levels, as recommended in previous editions. Implied volatility is produced from, for instance, the Black–Scholes Model, when the model is solved for volatility rather than price, taking the market price as the given.

The stop level should be marked on your chart as a horizontal line as soon as an actual or theoretical transaction has been entered into, and it should be maintained until the transaction is closed, or until progressive stops (which we will explain in a moment) have been started in order to close it out. In the case of purchases, the stop level ordinarily will be at the indicated distance below the last previous Minor Bottom. In the case of short sales, it ordinarily would be at the indicated distance above the last Minor Top.

To determine the position of this stop level, simply figure what the percentage distance would amount to at the price of the stock. If you are dealing with a stock selling at 30 and the stop distance comes out 10%, then allow 3 points under your last Minor Bottom.
End Quote.

A hand tailored method for determining filters

This procedure can undoubtedly be improved upon. The use of "sensitivity" may be beyond the patience of the modern reader. Implied volatility is not so farfetched, but depends on an option series. So the instrument volatility could be used. I would opt for a 23 day moving average of actual volatility. I am not competely happy with an inflexible table and generally for my own purposes try to hand tailor the parameter.

As I remarked (implied) earlier in this discussion I think it is quite possible that this filter might vary according to market conditions. That is, it might be 5% during the early stages of a stock's trend and might expand to 7% during interim blow off stages. This is a speculation on my part as I have not done any specific research on variable filters, but I have seen filters which worked to perfection in some markets malfunction in other markets. Once again this emphasizes the particularity of every market condition. The past never repeats exactly.

As they say, you can never step into the same river twice, and the ship always sails on a different sea.

Chapter 5

Step by Step Illustration of the Marking of Basing Points

The three-days-away procedure is not easily absorbed for some reason; bright graduate students wrestle with its details. The following charts walk the reader through the process. BP indicates a Basing Point. Obviously that is not known at the moment it occurs. BPC marks a Basing Point Candidate day. Obviously every Basing Point was a BPC before it was confirmed. In the days that follow a BPC "N" (No) marks days which are not "away" and "Y" (Yes) marks days which are valid away days: Again, those days completely out of the range of the BPC in the direction of the trend.

Figure 6. Chart BP 1.

In this chart we see a high made (6th) after a strong surge. This is both the wave high and the beginning of the down wave. Each day after this high day is a Basing Point Candidate. On the 14th a low is made which is the last in the downwave. We don't know this at the time, actually. But the next day a higher low is made; but, as marked by the N, it is not "away." That is, once again, it is within the range of the Basing Point day. The following two days are away and are marked Y. The following day returns to the Basing Point day range and is not away, and is marked with N. The day after (22nd) is away meaning that the 23rd the stop will be moved to x% under the low of the Basing Point day.

Note that no effort has been made to indicate the precise price level of the stop -- that only the concept is illustrated. The stop level is carefully placed on Chart Figure 201.1.1, Version 2. (3)

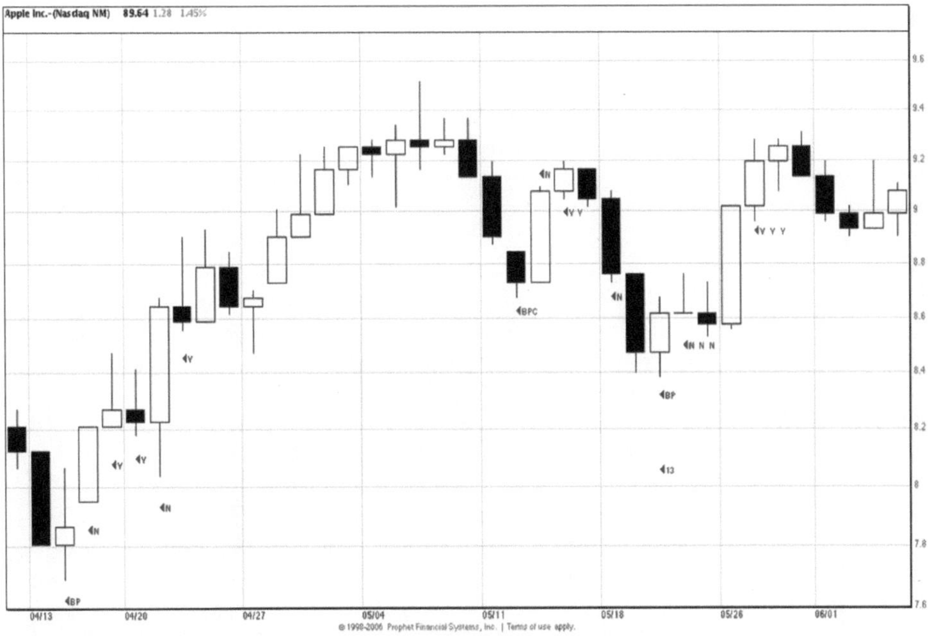

Figure 7. Chart BP 2

In this chart we see a strong advance ending the 6th which is also the beginning of the downwave. We will pass over the first part of the chart for the moment. The downwave is marked by several strong down days ending with a gap. The next day is a strong recovery and we immediately mark the gap day as a Basing Point Candidate. Two Y days follow almost confirming our gap day as the Basing Point. But the next day is a running down day, and it is followed by another run day down. The next day marked BP is a lower low and the beginning of the upwave although we don't know it at the time. We must examine the following days to determine that. Three days follow which are not away. Then three away days quickly follow. After the third of these the stop is raised to x% under the Basing Point day.

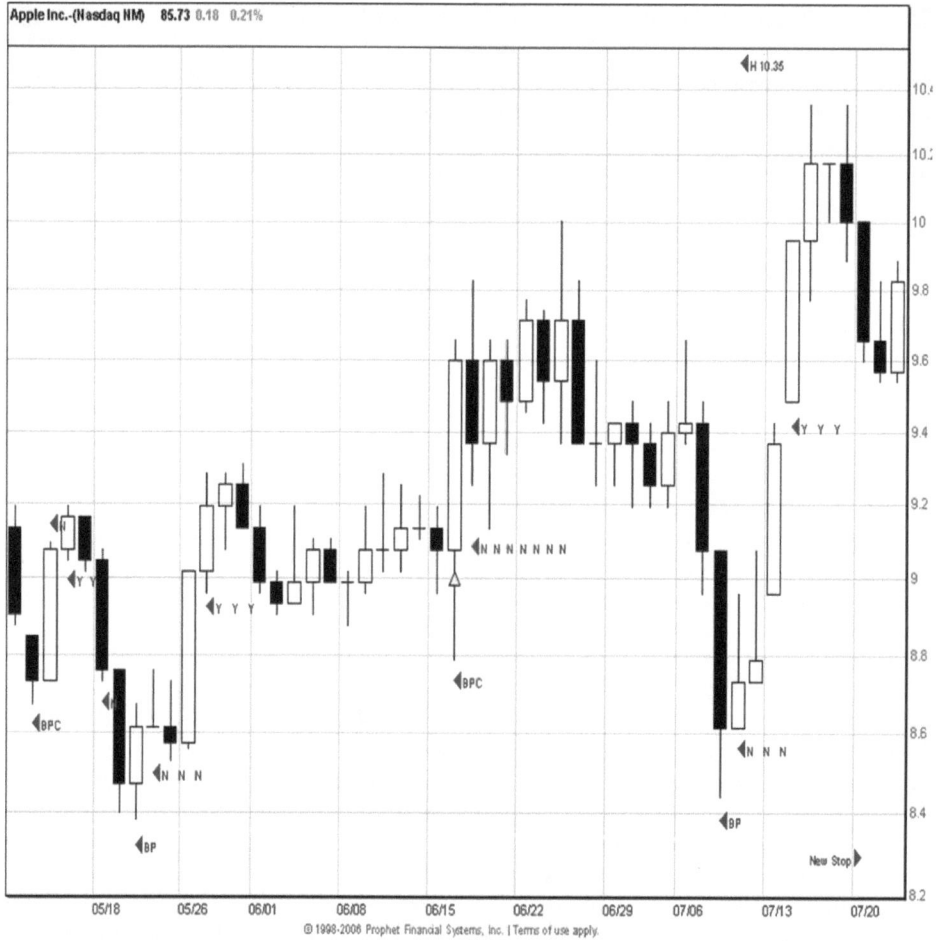

Figure 8. Chart BP 3

In the price action immediately after Chart BP 2 the price drifts sideways till we have long outside day, marked as BPC. This day is so long that 15 days elapse before a true Basing Point is made at a lower low the 9th. And we do not know that fact until 6 days have passed. Thus the Basing Point Candidate (BPC) is not confirmed, but washed out by the lower low before a later Basing Point is confirmed.

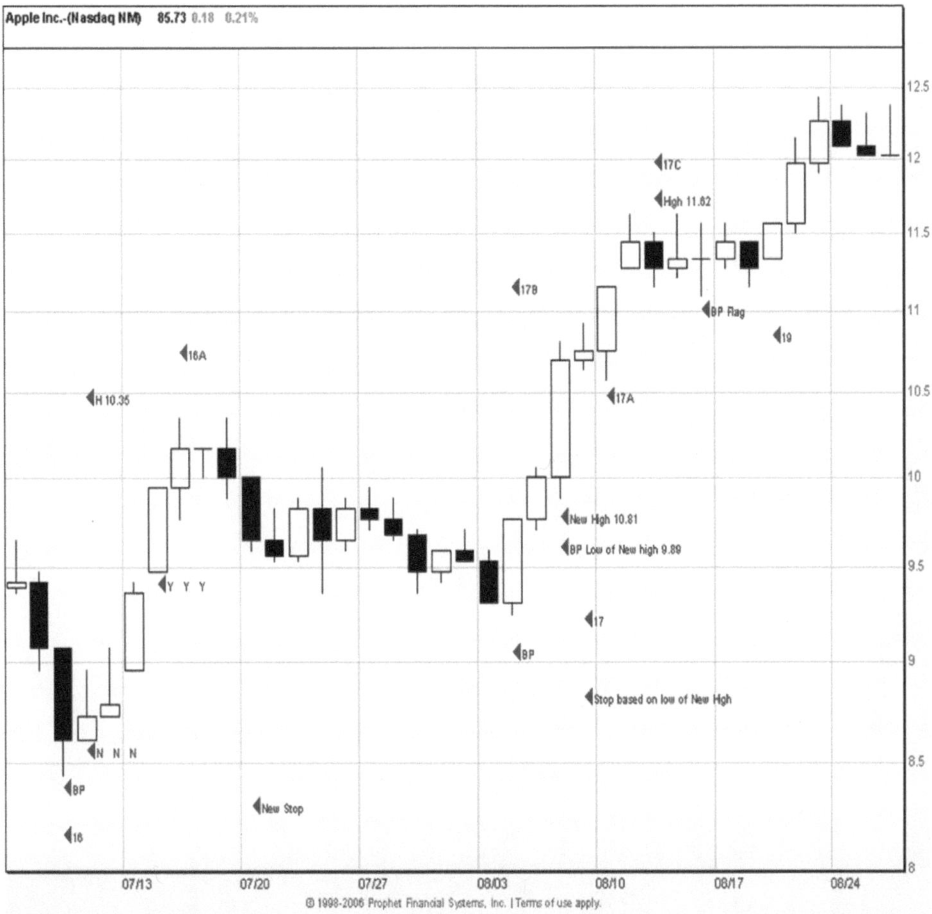

Figure 9. Chart BP 4

In this chart we have another instance of how a Basing Point may be set. Looked at on the longer term charts the running prices from the 15th are clearly seen as a flagpole. One of the marks of a flagpole is that it is not followed by a downwave, but by a "flag" which flies from the flagpole. When the price breaks out of the flag formation we may take the low of the flag as the new Basing Point when three-days-away have been made from the high of the flag formation. This same procedure may be used for a rectangle or consolidation formation which follows a surge in prices. In this chart we set a Basing Point the 4th based on a wave low, then we set another Basing Point at the low of the flag. In both cases we are following Variant 1 of the procedure. The notes on new highs in this chart are explained in the next chart caption.

Figure 10. Chart BP 5

In Chart BP 5 we examine the same period and formation as Chart BP 4. The difference here is that we are now looking at the setting of Basing Points using new highs. When a new high is made which exceeds the previous wave high by 3% the Basing Point may be moved to the low of the new high day. We may also use this rule when a price surge makes a new high (3%, A) and then runs to another new high (B 3% greater than A). Here we see how setting stops with Variant 2 of the procedure moves the stops faster and higher. This rule kicks in at numbers with alphabetics, 16A, 17A, etc.

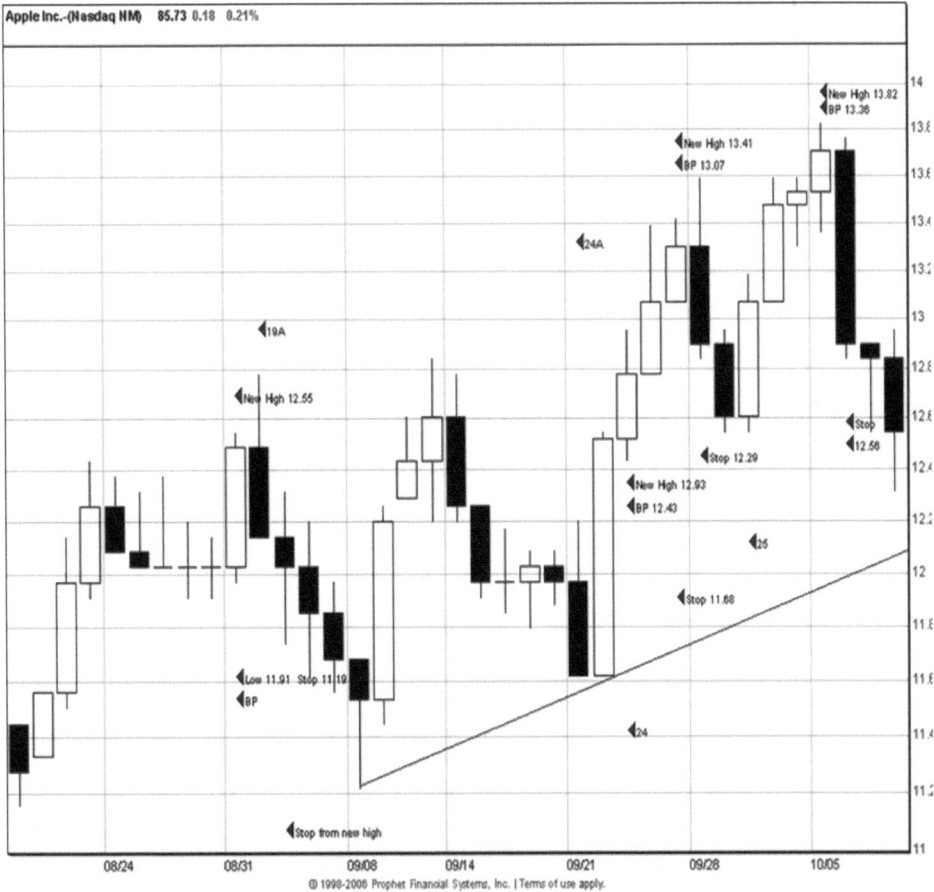

Figure 11. Chart BP 6

Once again in Chart BP 6 the difference in the two Basing Point determination methods is illustrated, and Variant 2 seizes a greater profit than Variant 1. The wide angle view of these events is in Figure 201.1.1 (3) and 201.1.1 (v2) (4)

As this close examination shows the procedure may be run with little if any qualitative judgment required in most cases. As in the case of the one armed economist, trade offs always exist between the rigid and rigorous use of algorithmic procedures and the more sensitive method of varying tactics judgmentally. Rigid rules vs discretion is both a theoretical and a practical question. And it will never be settled. The practitioner must settle the question for himself. This he may do by tracking his actual results when confronted with the opportunity (or pressure or necessity) of departing from the algorithmic procedure.

The procedure for bear markets is a mirror image of the above, with the same disclaimers and caveats.

Chapter 6

How the Procedure Worked in the Great Bear Market of 2008-09

Real time examples of shorting the Dow -- January '08 to March '09

Hundreds –perhaps thousands—of systems are sold in the marketplace. Without exception they report generating profits approaching the unbelievable – hundreds of percentages. Almost without exception these profits are the results of back tests and paper trading. Naturally I roll my eyes and throw these accounts into the trash. And, for my own part, I decline to participate in hype and misleading promotion. So it is with some hesitation that I cite the record of Magee's procedure produced in real time in actual markets. But only because of the context of hype in talking about systems. The record for this procedure was produced in real time and is verifiable in the letters posted on the internet in real time at the time under actual market conditions.

In brief the edwards-magee.com newsletter liquidated longs and went short the Dow Jones Industrials in January 2008 at the price of 12603.04. It remained short through the March 2009 bottom – 6133.09 gross Dow points.

Here is a picture of the market at the top in 2007:

Figure 12. The market top in the Dow, 2007, a weekly candlestick chart.

To the technician this is an obvious picture of a market top. The picture begins coming into focus along in September as the market begins to swing broadly sideways. But the analysis has been progressing as the chart developed. All of the drawn trendlines are significant, and in March and August clear Basing Points are made. What is interesting here is that we cannot see the right hand side of the chart, but we are already defining where we will exit the market. As the reader can see the process of identifying stop levels is relentless. A Basing Point is identified. The stop level is raised. The process never stops, and the method itself assures that we will not be long Enron or WorldCom – or an extended bear market.

Next is a daily picture of the top. The actual stop was calculated from the daily chart. I will not spend much text here on the difference between weekly and daily except to say that the use of weekly bars is inherently more conservative (of Dow Theory length as explored in my book *Sacred Chickens, The Holy Grail and Dow Theory*) than daily bars. Daily bars are more sensitive and cause quicker signals.

Figure 13. Daily basis chart of the 2007 market top.

In this chart the stop has not been hit yet, but a higher Basing Point has been created in October. The final stop is calculated from the Basing Point using a 5% filter: 12603.04. Let us emphsize that concept. The right side of the chart is absent. But the Basing Point method has identified stop levels which will indicate that the trend has changed. When we see the continuation of this chart it will be obvious to the dimmest trader (except for mutual fund managers) that the trend has changed, and that it is too late to catch the change.

In the next chart we see the completion of the top and the true beginning of the Bush Bear Market.

Figure 14. Completion of the top and beginning of the Bear Market. Stop hit.

In January of 2008 we see the stop hit that was calculated from the October Basing Point. And what happens immediately? A Basing Point is identified to protect the short sale. It is labeled BP1 (being the first Bear Market Basing Point) and is in November 2007. The Basing Point ratchets down in May 2008. While the rest of the mutual fund, hedge fund world is asleep, thinking that the rally from March to May is a resumption of the bull market. We Magee technicians have known for months that the market topped in the summer of 2007.

If we knew that why didn't we short it then? We shorted at 12603.04. Why didn't we short at 14000? Simple. We did not have definitive proof that the trend had changed. We could have used Variant 2 and been stopped out sooner. But we didn't. Because we considered Variant 1 inherently more conservative. Conservative investors win over the long term. Look at the record of the Dow Theory if you don't believe that.

So I have presented the big picture here of what was happening in the market. How about a picture of the actual decision and particular letter which put the edwards-magee.com short? I thought you'd never ask. Here it is, a snapshot of the letter from January 2008.

Figure 15. From the January 2008 edwards-magee.com letter.

Here is the text which went with this chart:

"January 11 2008 At the tipping point? At the bungee point? Is there a point?

Indeed. More points than an eight point buck. Point 1. Stop taken out. Point 2. Theoretical question about placement of stop. Usually in a sideways pattern the stop will be set below the bottom of the entire pattern. Using the basing point routine we computed the last stop here. We could do a lot more head scratching here but net net (point) that system is on the sidelines. We always believe in seasoning algorithmic systems with a little judgement. So we don't really think the pattern is complete until the August low is solidly taken out. But (or and) Dow Theory is out and the punditry is braying for a bear market -- but then they have been for months."

The original of this letter may be found on the net at: http://www.edwards-magee.com/nf08/08apr.html. Letters written before and after this letter will give the reader a thorough display of our thinking and analysis.

The reader may also be interested in another letter written later in the year as the nature of the threat became clearer.
March 28 2008 we wrote the following letter:

03/28/2008 1:15 PM EDT (4 years, weekly)

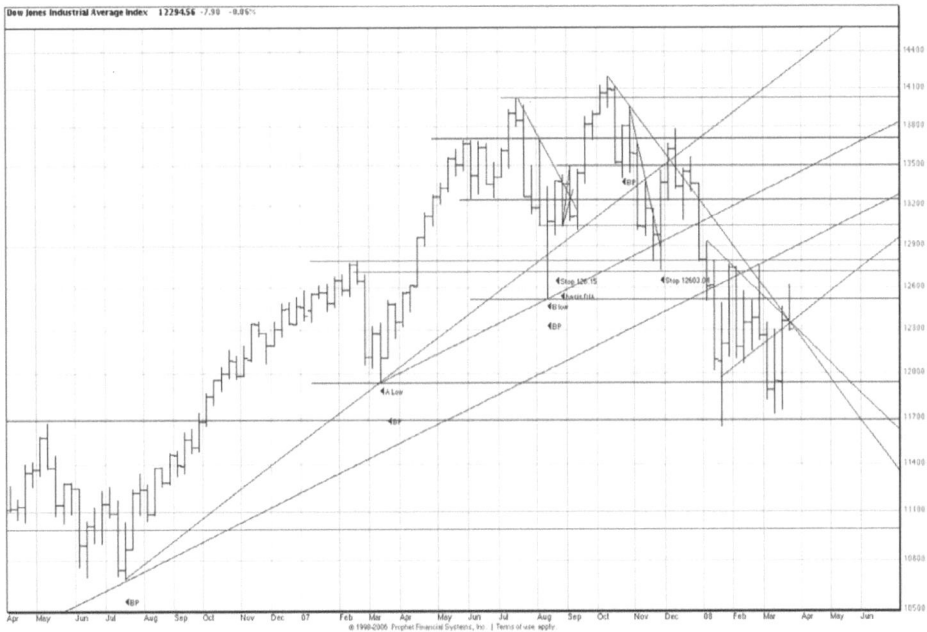

Figure 16. Head and shoulders in March 28 2008.

"March 28 2008 Dow 16000? Flying-Vampire Pigs, Levitating pundits....
Random egg attacks.

Note "A low" and "B low". If this yearlong formation is a massive top (perhaps
a double headed head and shoulders) and A low is its lower boundary then
a low of 9680 is predicted. If B low is the defining point the predicted low
is 10836. Remember Nils Bohr and the difficulty of forecasting. Again, it
is not necessary to believe this scenario to know how to bet. The Dow is in
a six month downtrend, the last 2 1/2 months of which are sideways, with
lower highs in the sidetrend."

This might appear prescient, but it is only the application of methods every
technician knows from reading *Technical Analysis of Stock Trends, 9th
Ed.* I am completely accustomed to see my students make analyses of this
kind. Of course what occurred after this chart was one of the historic bear
markets:

Figure 17. The continuation of the Bush Bear Market, ending March 2009.
Weekly.

I will not belabor the reader with the protracted continuation of this story
(all online at edwards-magee.com). In fact Variant 2 of the Basing Points
procedure went long March 23 2009. Variant 1 waited until August to get
long. While this was the action of the Basing Point procedure other methods
put the edwards-magee.com letter long in March and April in individual
stocks and gold.

Appendix Drill

Exercise in Applying The Procedure

Stair Stops and Basing Points

It is through back study that we learn the language of the market and observe how our method would have functioned if we had known then what we know now. This kind of study is indispensable and invaluable. But the market happening now, right this minute, before tomorrow's New York Times, presents that most disturbing aspect of all human experience. We have no idea how it will turn out.

Or do we have no idea? In fact, not to go too deeply into philosophy and probabilities, we do have an idea how it will turn out: Because of the first law of trends: The present trend will continue. And like the camel tracks in the Arabian sands it is likely the tracks will continue going where they are going until they give some sign they have finished their trek.

Uncertainty

A little thought will deal with the concept of uncertainty. The entry to a trade can have three results. The price can go up, in which case after some progress the stop can be raised locking in the profit. Or the price can go sideways, resulting in no loss or profit. Or the price can decline to our first stop, computed and placed when we entered the trade. This will terminate our position with a known loss.

The Trend Tends to Continue

The most important rule of trend following is: The trend tends to continue.

This being true, if we take our position in the direction prices are going and progressively advance our stops according to market action we should realize a successful operation. And, as there is always more uncertainty at the inception of a trade or investment, should the prices go against the trade the stop we set upon entering will end our participation in the trade before prices have gone from $95 to $.06 as they did with Enron in 2002 (Chart 10). Astounding as it might seem, as Enron was in free fall, professional managers and investors who could not read the handwriting on the wall or follow the camel tracks actually increased their investments in the falling duck (turkey?).

Long-term trend following investors buy strength, not weakness. As we have seen, buying weakness may result in cornering the market for Enron (or WorldCom).

The Stair Stops Exercise

In this exercise we are presented with the real life problem of not being able to see the right hand side of the chart. It is, as Columbus discovered, terra incognita. So how are we to identify a trend and stick to it until it has changed? And how are we to deal with the inevitable reactions against the trend? Surprisingly, there are several simple methods. Of these the method I have called "StairStops" is, I think, the prototype of all trend following techniques.

In the following case I illustrate an example of the principle of buying strength and sticking with the trend until the procedure indicates the trend has exhausted itself. While trend lines are used as a general guide the more important technique in this example is the use of what Magee called "Basing Points."

Basing Points are the important lows in retracements which an investor may use as technical points on which to base stops. Details of their identification and use follow.

Stair Stops and the three-days-away rule

To identify a Basing Point in actual trading, the trader watches each day in a retracement until the reaction ends and prices begin to advance again. Each day after the low day is checked to determine that it is out of the range of the low day. That is, if the high of the low day was 10 the day under consideration must have a low of 10.1 or higher. When three such days have occurred the Basing Point is established and the stop may be raised to 5% (or x%, a parameter) under that point.

Stair Stops

The reader should now examine Chart 24 and

guesstimate where he might have gone long, and where he might have or have not liquidated his trade. At this point in the chart the reader should examine the chart to determine whether he believes that the issue should be held, or sold, or hedged or whether the investment should be increased. These decisions should be noted. In view of our discussions in the book up to this point the reader should want to use a ruler. Trend lines should be marked as well as support and resistance lines. Do this before going to the next page. Notice the way the price moves in waves. Mark wave highs and wave lows.

Since it is important that the reader see the problem before the solution, the problem must be on the odd page, necessitating the insertion of a "marking time" page. On the marking time page I insert art which is not only intended to delight the reader but also to act on his subconscious mind to make him a better investor.

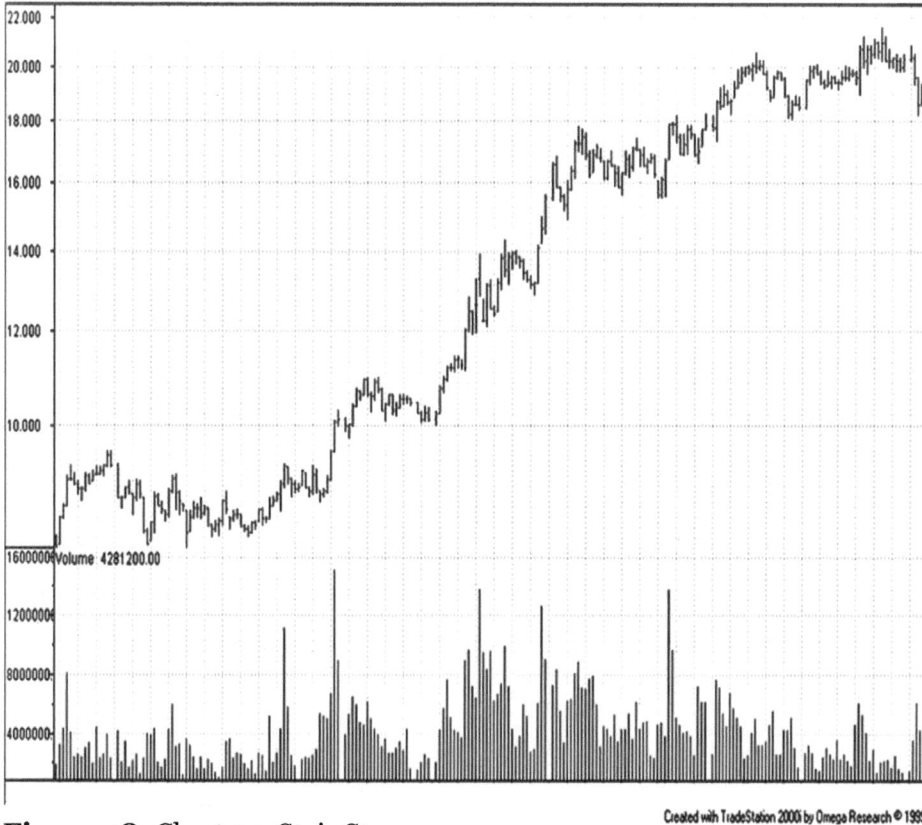

Figure 18. Chart 24 Stair Stops

The reader should now analyze this chart to determine where he would have gone long; where the support and resistance and trendlines are; and what should be done at this point – sell, hold or short. Make this analysis of this chart before turning to the next page.

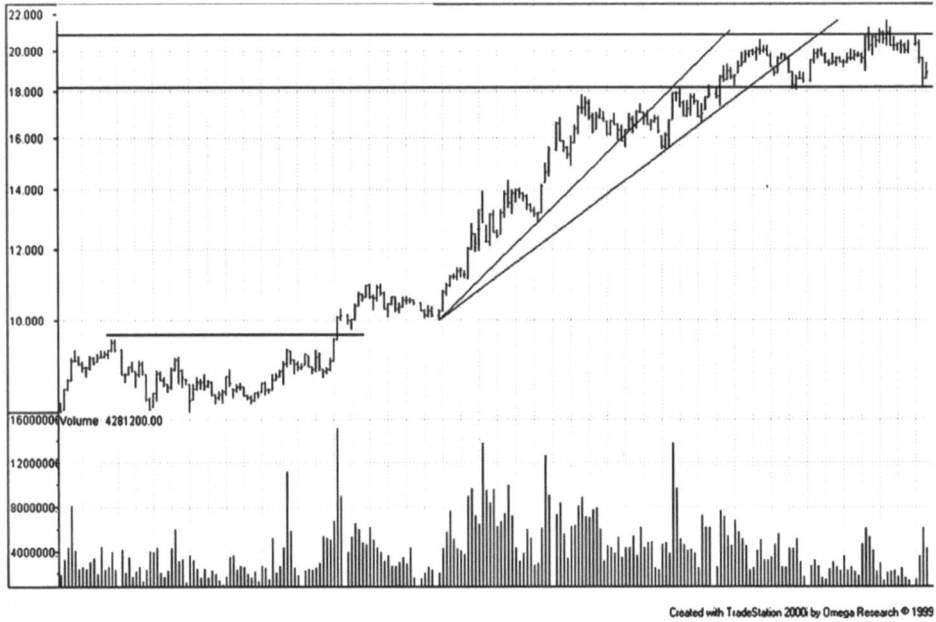

Created with TradeStation 2000i by Omega Research © 1999

Figure 19. Chart 25

Here is an example of a simple and perfectly adequate analysis of the issue in Chart 24. An analysis like this serves the purpose of technical investing: follow the trend without being shaken out and do not surrender back in a trice profits gained through much patience.

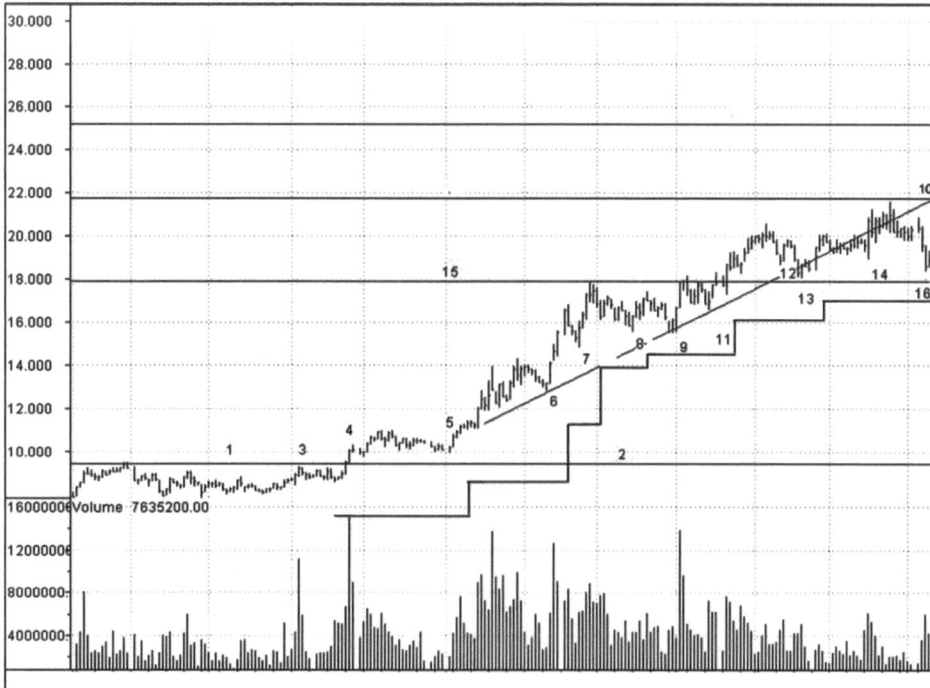

Figure 20. Chart 26

Now let us examine a procedure which is extremely powerful. John Magee called it the three-days-away Procedure, and I call it the StairStops Procedure. As the reader will see from the chart here and its key, a supremely rational and effective method may be used for buying, holding and selling almost any issue. Not every issue will lend itself to this method, but the principle is very like the principle underlying the Dow Theory. In this chart we have found the Basing Point using the three-days-away rule and then calculated a stop by using a filter of 6%. We indicate the level of the stop by the horizontal lines, which, when connected look like stair steps.

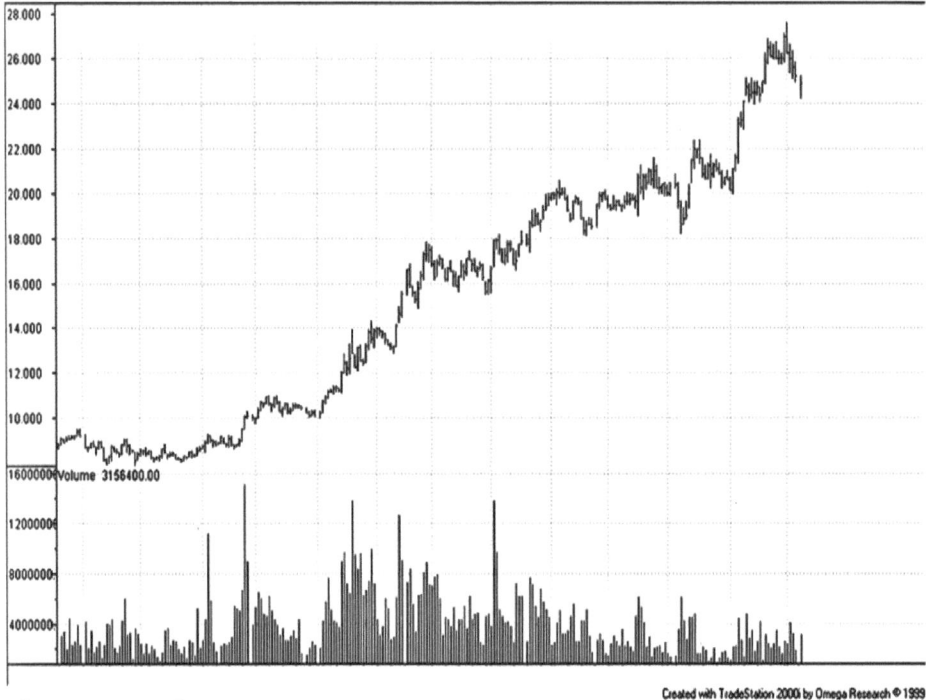

Figure 21. Chart 27

As will be seen in this chart the correct (actually, correct is a bad word; a better word is skillful) approach to the previous Chart 24 was to hold the position, or to increase the investment. The reader should now make the same evaluation of this chart before going to the next odd page. Should the position be held, increased, or liquidated? Mark the chart with trend lines and support and resistance lines and annotate it.

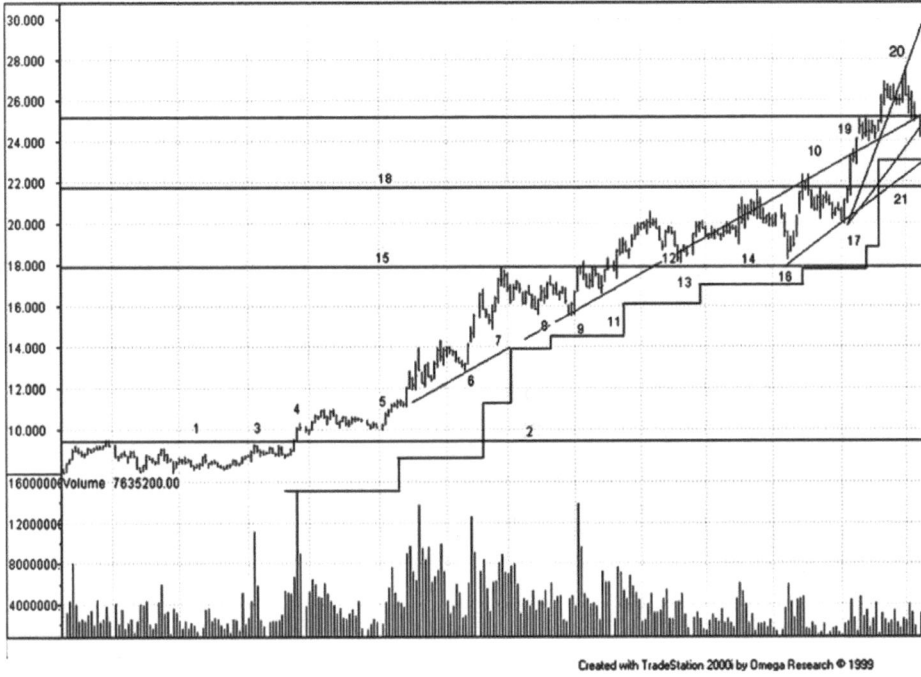

Figure 22. Chart 28

Illustrates the Stair Stops (three-days-away) Procedure using the two charts the Beginner has just analyzed.

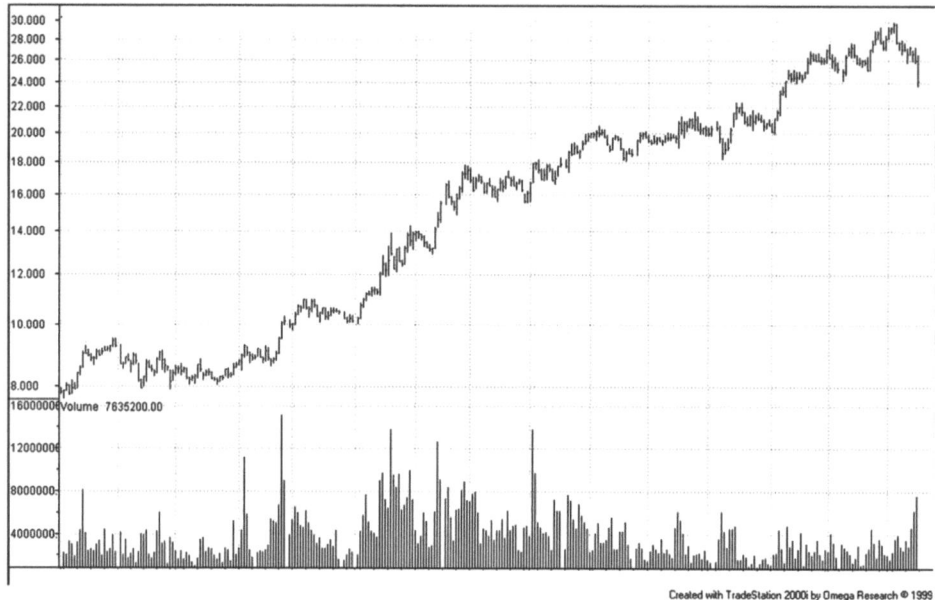

Figure 23. Chart 29

Once more the reader should make the same analysis of the chart, and annotate his observations and conclusions, now that he has seen a Basing Points analysis. Here is a recapitulation of the questions to ask:

Where are the support/resistance zones? Where is (are) the trendline or trendlines and where is the price in relationship to the trendlines? What is the relationship of volume to price? Is it kosher, or suspicious? Are the highs and lows in proper relationship? Does it smell right? And, most importantly, where are the Basing Points?

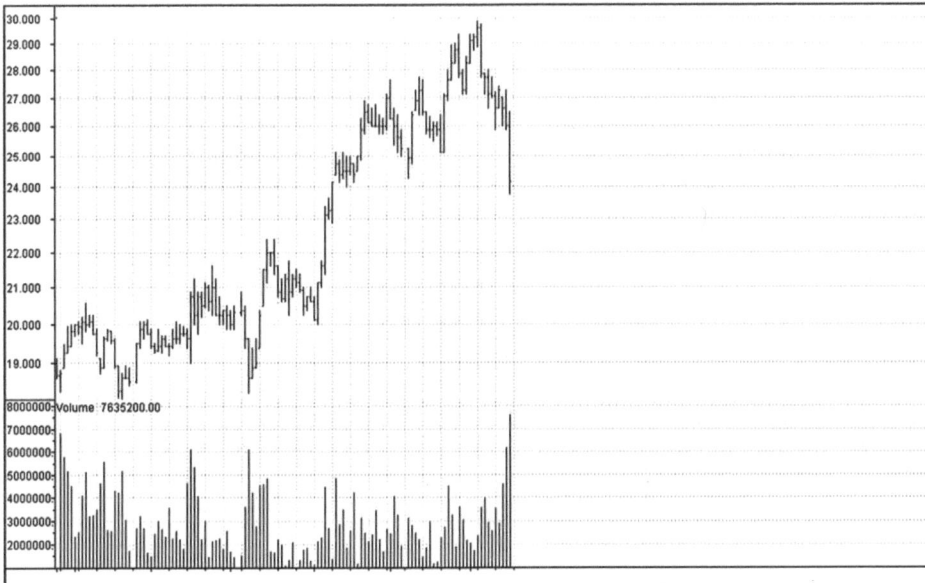

Figure 24. Chart 30

Here is a blow up of the end of the chart above. That chart may be analyzed using Basing Points and Stair Stops and also with conventional chart lines. In actual market action we will almost invariably want to examine the market close up before we make our final trading decision. What is the most important fact on the chart?

Figure 25. Chart 31

In Chart 30 (fig 24) the extreme range and extreme volume of the last day would strongly incline the trader to exit even if the stop were not hit.

Key to Case 1 Analysis

1. A rounding bottom, or perhaps a scallop
2. Resistance or breakout line
3. Wake up call on volume
4. Run Day, big volume; Breakout through line 2; Sure entry signal
5. First Basing Point (BP) Notice prior volume fall off in consolidation, and surge on run-day
6. BP
7. A weak BP (because of shallowness of retracement)
8. BP
9. Test of BP at 8
10. A trendline drawn after point 9
11. BP
12. BP candidate which fails 3 day rule
13. BP
14. A potential BP but not a very good one because new high has not been made from 13.
15. A support/resistance line
16. BP
17. BP
18. A resistance/support line.
19. Flag which becomes BP
20. TL, but too steep to last
21. Trendline
22. BP
23. Trendline
24. BP
25. BP
26. Horizontal trend line
27. BP at 25 is 26.75 (stop 25.15) Stopped out at 25.15

UNMARKED CHARTS WHICH MAY BE USED FOR PRACTICE IN MARKING BASING POINTS
The answers to these exercises will be found on the www. edwards-magee.com website.

Figure 26

Apple Computer Inc.-(Nasdaq NM)   76.38 -1.23   -1.58%

@ 1998-2006 Prophet Financial Systems, Inc. | Terms of use apply.

Figure 27

Figure 28

Figure 29

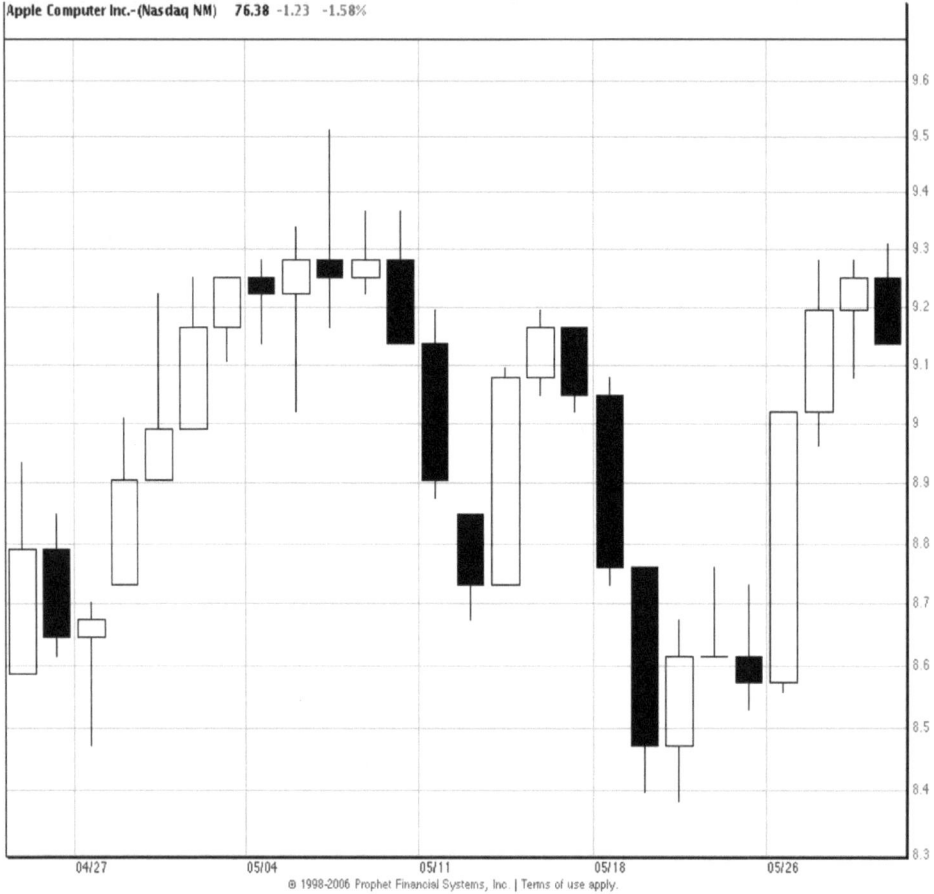

Figure 30

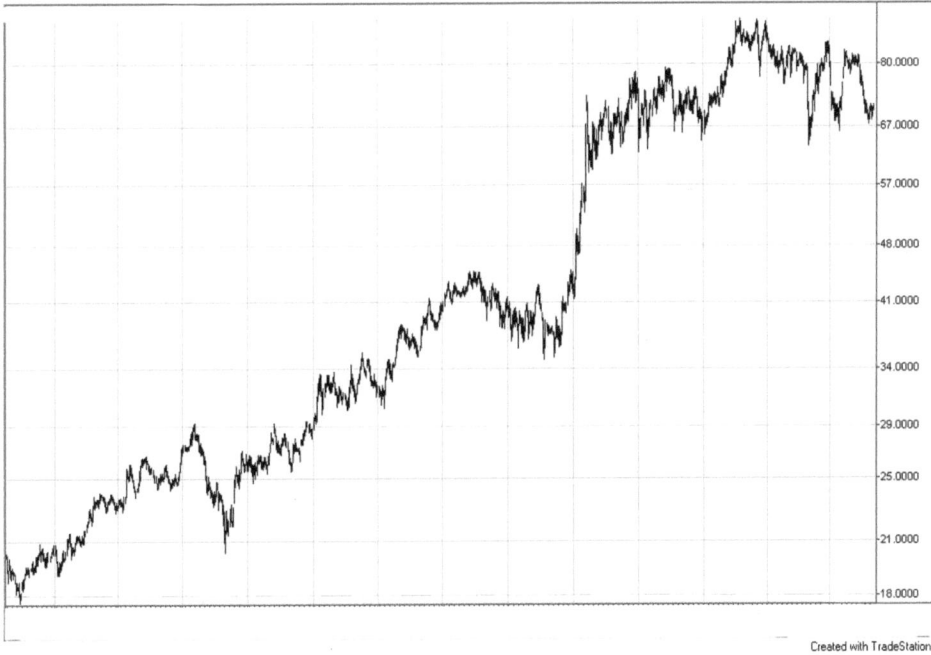

Figure 31

Enso: What To Think About While Putting

Glossary

ACCUMULATION-The first phase of a Bull Market. The period when farsighted investors begin to buy shares from discouraged or distressed sellers. Financial reports are usually at their worst and the public is completely disgusted with the stock market. Volume is only moderate, but beginning to increase on the rallies.

AREA PATTERN-When a stock or commodity's upward or downward momentum has been temporarily exhausted, the ensuing sideways movement in the price usually traces out a design or arrangement of form called an Area Pattern. The shape of some of these Area Patterns, or Formations, have predictive value under certain conditions.

(See also Ascending Triangle, Broadening Formations, Descending Triangle, Diamond, Flag, Head-and-Shoulders, Inverted Triangle, Pennant, Rectangle, Right-Angle Triangles, Symmetrical Triangles, and Wedges.)

ASCENDING (UP) TRENDLINE-The advancing wave in a stock or commodity price is composed of a series of waves. When the bottoms of these waves form on, or very close to, an upward slanting straight line, a basic Ascending or Up Trendline is formed.

ASCENDING TRIANGLE-One of a class of Area Patterns called Right-Angle Triangles. The class is distinguished by the fact that one of the two boundary lines is practically horizontal while the other slants toward it. If the top line is horizontal and the lower slants upward to an intersection point to the right, the resulting Area Pattern is called an Ascending Triangle. The implication is bullish, with the expectant breakout though the horizontal line. Measuring Formula: Add the broadest part of triangle to the breakout point.

AVERAGES-See Dow-Jones Industrial Averages, Moving Averages, Dow-Jones, Transportation Averages, and Dow-Jones Utility Averages.

BAR CHART-Also called a Line Chart and sometimes a Vertical Chart. A graphic representation of prices using a vertical bar to connect the highest price in the time period to the lowest price. Opening prices are noted with a small horizontal line to the left. Closing prices are shown with a small horizontal line to the right. Bar charts can be constructed for any time period in which prices are available. The most common time periods found in bar charts are hourly, daily, weekly and monthly. However, with the growing number of personal computers and the availability of "real time" quotes, it is not unusual for traders to use some period of minutes to construct a bar chart.

BASING POINT-The price level (wave high, wave low) in the chart which determines where a stop-loss point is placed. (I.e. the point from which it is calculated.) As technical conditions change, the Basing Point, and stops, can be advanced (in a rising market), or lowered (in a falling market). (See Progressive Stops.)

BEAR MARKET-In its simplest form, a Bear Market is a period when prices are primarily declining, usually for a long period of time. Bear Markets generally consist of three phases. The first phase is distribution, the second is panic, and the third is akin to a washout, where those investors who have held through the first two phases, finally give up and liquidate.

BLOW-OFF-See Climactic Top.

BOTTOM-See Ascending Triangle, Dormant Bottom, Double Bottom, Head-and-Shoulders Bottom, Rounding Bottom, and Selling Climax.

BOUNDARY-The edges of a pattern.

BOWL-See Rounding Bottom.

BREAKAWAY GAP-The hole or gap in the chart prices created when a stock or commodity breaks out of an Area Pattern. The low of the breakout day does not touch the high of the previous day.

BREAKOUT-When a stock or commodity exits an area pattern. And, when price crosses a trendline.

BROADENING FORMATION-Sometimes called Inverted Triangles, these are formations which start with narrow fluctuations that widen out between diverging, rather than converging, boundary lines

BROADENING TOP-An Area Reversal Pattern which may evolve in any one of three forms, comparable in shape, respectively, to inverted Symmetrical, Ascending, or Descending Triangles. Unlike Triangles, however, the Tops and Bottoms of these patterns do not necessarily stop at clearly marked diverging boundary lines. Volume, rather than diminishing in triangles, tends to be unusually high and irregular throughout pattern construction. No Measuring Formula is available.

BUBBLE-An overblown overextended market full of hot air and dangerously inflated prices.

BULL MARKET-A period when prices are primarily rising, normally for an extended period. Usually, but not always, divisible into three phases. The first phase is accumulation. The second phase is one of fairly steady advance with increasing volume. The third phase is marked by considerable activity as the public begins to recognize and attempt to profit from the rising market.

BULL TRAP-A price advance over previous highs, usually those of an area pattern, which cause traders to get long. Prices then fall trapping those who bought the "breakout."

BUY-AND-HOLD-An investment strategy which plans to hold purchases forever, or until they go bankrupt. (See the buy-and-hold strategy for Enron).

CANDIDATE DAY-A day which is marked as a potential Basing Point day. After three days away it becomes a Basing Point.

CAPITULATION-The bottom of a bear market when sellers who have suffered price deterioration throw in their hands (and their stock). Usually marked by extreme volume and price decline

CLEAN-OUT DAY-See Selling Climax.

CLIMACTIC TOP-A sharp advance, accompanied by extraordinary volume, i.e., much larger volume than the normal increase, which signals the final "blow-off" of the trend, followed by either a Reversal, or at least by a period of stagnation, formation of Consolidation Pattern, or a Correction.

CLIMAX DAY-See One-Day Reversal.

CLIMAX, SELLING-See Selling Climax.

CLOSING PRICE-The last sale price of the trading session for a stock. In a commodity, it represents an official price determined from a range of prices deemed to have traded at or on the close; also called a settlement price.

CLOSING THE GAP-When a stock or commodity returns to a previous gap and retraces the range of the gap. Also called covering the gap or filling the gap. (See also Gap.)

COMPLEX HEAD-AND-SHOULDERS-Also called Multiple Head-and-Shoulders It is a Head-and-Shoulders Pattern with more than one right and left shoulder and/or head. (See also Head and-Shoulders.)

CONFIRMATION-In a pattern, it is the point at which a stock or commodity exits an Area Pattern in the expected direction by an amount of price and volume sufficient to meet minimum pattern requirements for a bonafide breakout. In the Dow Theory, it means both the Industrial Average and the Transportation Average have registered new highs or lows during the same advance or decline. If only one of the Averages establishes a new high (or low) and the other one does not, it would be a non-confirmation, or Divergence. This is also true of oscillators. To confirm a new high (or low) in a stock or commodity, an oscillator needs to reach a new high (or low) as well. Failure of the oscillator to confirm a new high (or low) is called a Divergence and would be considered an early indication of a potential Reversal in direction.

CONGESTION-The sideways trading from which Area Patterns evolve. Not all Congestion periods produce a recognizable pattern, however.

CONSOLIDATION PATTERN-Also called a Continuation Pattern, it is an Area Pattern which breaks out in the direction of the previous trend. (See also Ascending Triangle, Descending Triangle, Hag, Head-and-Shoulders Continuation, Pennant, Rectangle, Scallop, and Symmetrical Triangle.)

CONTINUATION GAP-See Runaway Gap.

CONTINUATION PATTERN-See Consolidation Pattern.

CONVERGENT PATTERN (TREND)-Those patterns with upper and lower boundary lines which meet, or converge, at some point if extended to the right. (See also Ascending Triangle, Descending Triangle, Symmetrical Triangle, Wedges, and Pennants.)

CORRECTION-A move in a commodity or stock which is opposite to the prevailing trend, but not sufficient to change that trend. Called a rally in a downtrend and a reaction in an uptrend. In the Dow Theory, a Correction is a Secondary Trend against the Primary Trend, which usually lasts from three weeks to three months and retraces from one-third to two-thirds of the preceding swing in the Primary Direction.

COVERING THE GAP-See Closing the Gap.

DAILY RANGE-The difference between the high and low price during one trading day.

DEMAND-Buying interest for a stock at a given price.

DESCENDING TRENDLINE-The declining wave in a stock or commodity is composed of a series of ripples. When the tops of these ripples form on, or very close to, a downward slanting straight line, a basic Descending or Down Trendline is formed.

DESCENDING TRIANGLE-One of a class of Area Patterns called Right-Angle Triangles. The class is distinguished by the fact that one of the two boundary lines is practically horizontal while the other slants toward it. If the bottom line is horizontal and the upper slants downward to an intersection point to the right, the resulting Area Pattern is called a Descending Triangle. The implication is Bearish, with the expectant breakout through the flat (horizontal) side. Minimum Measuring Formula: Add the broadest part of the Triangle to the breakout point.

DIAMOND-Usually a Reversal Pattern, but it will also be found as a Continuation Pattern. It could be described as a Complex Head-and-Shoulders Pattern with a V-shaped (bent) Neckline, or a Broadening Pattern which, after two or three swings, changes into a regular Triangle. The overall shape is a four-point Diamond. Since it requires a fairly active market, it is more often found at Major Tops. Many Complex Head-and-Shoulders Tops are borderline Diamond Patterns. The major difference is in the right side of the pattern. It should clearly show two converging lines with diminishing volume as in a Symmetrical Triangle. Minimum Measuring Formula: Add the greatest width of the pattern to the breakout point.

DISTRIBUTION-The first phase of a Bear Market, which really begins in the last stage of a Bull Market. The period when farsighted investors sense that the market has outrun its fundamentals and begin to unload their holdings at an increasing pace. Trading volume is still high; however, it tends to diminish on rallies. The public is still active, but beginning to show signs of caution as hoped-for profits fade away.

DIVERSIFICATION-The concept of placing your funds in different industry groups and investment vehicles to spread risk. Not to put all your financial eggs in one basket.

DIVIDENDS-A share of the profits-in cash or stock equivalent which is paid to stockholders.

DORMANT BOTTOM-A variation of a Rounding (Bowl) Bottom, but in an extended, flat-bottomed form. It usually appears in "thin" stocks, (i.e., those issues with a small number of shares outstanding) and characteristically will show lengthy periods during which no sales will be registered for days at a time. The chart will appear "fly-specked" due to the missing days. The technical implication is for an upside breakout.

DOUBLE BOTTOM-Reversal Pattern. A Bottom formed on relatively high volume which is followed by a rally (of at least 15%), and then a second Bottom (possibly rounded) at the same level (plus or minus 3%) as the first Bottom on lower volume. A rally back though the apex of the intervening rally confirms the Reversal. More than a month should separate the two Bottoms. Minimum Measuring Formula: Take the distance from the lowest bottom to the apex of the intervening rally and add it to the apex.

DOUBLE TOP-A high-volume Top is formed, followed by a reaction (of at least 15%) on diminishing activity. Another rally back to the previous high (plus or minus 3%) is made, but on lower volume than the first high. A decline through the low of the reaction confirms the Reversal. The two highs should be more than a month apart. Minimum Measuring Formula: Add to the breakout point the distance from the highest peak to the low of the reaction. Also called an "M" Formation.

DOUBLE TRENDLINE-When two relatively close Parallel Trendlines are needed to define the true trend pattern. (See also Trendline.)

DOW-JONES INDUSTRIAL AVERAGE-Developed by Charles Dow in 1885 to study market trends. Originally composed of 14 companies (12 railroads and 2 industrials), the rails, by 1897, were separated into their own Average, and 12 industrial companies of the day were selected for the Industrial Average. The number was increased to 20 in 1916, and to 30 in 1928. The stocks included in this Average have been changed from time to time to keep the list up-to-date, or to accommodate a merger. The only original issue still in the Average is General Electric.

DOW-JONES TRANSPORTATION AVERAGE-Established at the turn of the century with the new Industrial Average, it was originally called the Rail Average and was composed of 20 railroad companies. With the advent of the airlines industry, the Average was updated in 1970 and the name changed to Transportation Average.

DOW-JONES UTILITY AVERAGE-In 1929, utility companies were dropped from the Industrial Average and a new Utility Average of 20 companies was created. In 1938, the number of issues was reduced to the present 15.

DOWNGAP-Also, amongst some lexicographers down-gap – a fall in prices which leaves open space between bars.

DOWNTICK-A securities transaction which is at a price that is lower than the preceding transaction.

DOWNTREND-See Descending Trendline and Trend.

DOWNWAVE-(down-wave) A downtrend in prices which is more or less regular in its descending pattern of lower highs and lower lows.

DRAWDOWN-Decline in account equity from a peak value.

END RUN-When a breakout of a Symmetrical Triangle Pattern reverses its direction and trades back through axis Support (if an up-side breakout) or Resistance (if a downside breakout), it is termed an end run around the line, or end run for short. The term is sometimes used to denote breakout failure in general.

EQUILIBRIUM MARKET-A price area that represents a balance between demand and supply.

EXHAUSTION GAP-Relatively wide gap in the price of a stock or commodity which occurs near the end of a strong directional move in the price. These gaps are quickly closed, most often within two to five days, which helps to distinguish them from Runaway Gaps which are not usually covered for a considerable length of time. An Exhaustion Cap cannot be read as a Major Reversal, or even necessarily a Reversal. It signals a halt in the prevailing trend which is ordinarily followed by some sort of area pattern development.

FALSE BREAKOUT-(BULL TRAP, BEAR TRAP) A breakout which is confirmed but which quickly reverses and eventually leads the stock or commodity to a breakout in the opposite direction. Indistinguishable from premature breakout or genuine breakout when it occurs.

50-DAY MOVING AVERAGE LINE-Is determined by taking the closing price over the past 50 trading days and dividing by 50.

FLAG-A Continuation Pattern. A flag is a period of congestion, less than four weeks in duration, which forms after a sharp, near vertical, change in price. The upper and lower boundary lines of the pattern are parallel, though both may slant up, down or sideways. In an uptrend, the pattern resembles a Flag flying

from a mast, hence the name. Flags are also called Measuring or HalfMast Patterns because they tend to form at the midpoint of the rally or reaction. Volume tends to diminish during the formation, and increase on the breakout. Minimum Measuring Formula:
Add the distance from the breakout point, which started the preceding "Mast" rally or reaction, to the breakout point of the Flag.

FORMATION-See Area Pattern.

FRACTAL-Self similarity at all scales. Or, as example, fact that tick by tick price data looks the same as monthly data.

FUNDAMENTALS-Information on a stock pertaining to the business of the company and how it relates to earnings and dividends. In a commodity, it would be information on any factor which would affect supply or demand.

GAP-A hole in the price range which occurs when either: (a) the lowest price at which a stock or commodity is traded during any time period is higher than the highest price at which it was traded on the preceding time period, or (b) the highest price of one time period is lower than the lowest price of the preceding time period. When the ranges of the two time periods are plotted, they will not overlap or touch the same horizontal level on the chart-there will be a price gap between them. (See also Common or Area Gap, ExDividend Gap, Breakaway Gap, Runaway Gap, Exhaustion Gap and Island Reversal.)

HEAD-AND-SHOULDERS   PATTERN-Although occasionally an Inverted Head-and-Shoulders Pattern (called a Consolidation Head-and-Shoulders) will form which is a Continuation Pattern, in its normal form, this pattern is one of the more common and more reliable of the Major Reversal Patterns. It consists of the following four elements (a Head-and-Shoulders Top will be described for illustration): (a) a rally which ends a more or less extensive advance on heavy volume, and which is then followed by a Minor Reaction on less volume. This is the left shoulder; (b) another high-volume advance which exceeds the high of the left shoulder, followed by another low-volume reaction which takes prices down to near the bottom of the preceding reaction, and below the top of the left shoulder high. This is the head; (c) a third rally, but on decidedly less volume than accompanied either of the first two advances, and which fails to exceed the high established on the head. This is the right shoulder; and (d) a decline through a line drawn across the proceeding two reaction lows (the neckline), and a close below that line equivalent to 3% of the stock's market price. This is the confirmation of the breakout. A Head-and-Shoulders Bottom, or any other combination Head-and-Shoulders Pattern, contains the same four elements. The main difference between a Top Formation and a Bottom Formation is in the volume patterns. The breakout in a Top can be on low volume. The breakout in a Bottom must show a "conspicuous burst of activity." Minimum Measuring Formula: Add the distance between the head and neckline to the breakout point.

HEAD-AND-SHOULDERS (KILROY) BOTTOM-Area Pattern which reverses a decline. (See also Head-and-Shoulders Pattern.)

HEAD-AND-SHOULDERS CONSOLIDATION-Area Pattern which continues the previous trend. (See also Head-and-Shoulders Pattern.)

HEAD-AND-SHOULDERS TOP-Area Pattern which reverses an advance. (See also Head-and-Shoulders Pattern.)

HEAVY VOLUME-The expression "heavy volume," as used by Edwards and Magee, means heavy only with respect to the recent volume of sales in the stock you are watching.

HEDGING-To try to lessen risk by making a counterbalancing investment. In a stock portfolio, an example of a hedge would be to buy 100 shares of XYZ stock, and to buy one put option of the same stock. The put would help protect against a decline in the stock, but it would also limit potential gains on the upside.

HIGHER HIGH HIGHER LOW-The wave pattern of a bull trend as price advances in waves.

HORIZONTAL CHANNEL-When the Tops of the rallies and Bottoms of the reactions form along lines which are horizontal and parallel to one another, the area in between is called a Horizontal Trend Channel. It may also be called a Rectangle during the early stages of formation.

HORIZONTAL TRENDLINE-A horizontal line drawn across either the Tops or Bottoms in a sideways trending market.

INDUSTRIAL AVERAGE-See Dow- Jones Industrial Average.

INSIDERS-Individuals who possess fundamental information likely to affect the price of a stock, but which is unavailable to the public. An example would be an individual who knows about a merger before it is announced to the public. Trading by insiders on this type of information is illegal.

INTERMEDIATE TREND-In Edwards and Magee, the term Intermediate or Secondary refers to a trend (or pattern indicating a trend) against the Primary (Major) Trend which is likely to last from three weeks to three months, and which may retrace one-third to two-thirds of the previous Primary Advance or Decline.

ISLAND REVERSAL-A compact trading range, usually formed after a fast rally or reaction, which is separated from the previous move by an Exhaustion Gap, and from the move in the opposite direction which follows by a Breakaway Gap. The result is an Island of prices detached by a gap before and after. If the trading range contains only one day, it is called a One-Day Reversal. The two gaps usually occur at approximately the same level. By itself, the pattern is not of major significance; but it does frequently send prices back for a complete retracement of the Minor Move which preceded it.

LEVERAGE-Using a smaller amount of capital to control an investment of greater value. For example, exclusive of interest and commission costs, if you buy a stock on 50% margin, you control $1 of stock for every 50 cents invested or leverage of 2-to-1.

LIMIT ORDER-A buy or sell order which is limited in some way, usually in price. For example, if you placed a limit order to buy IBM at 100, the broker would not fill the order unless he could do so at your price or better, i.e., at 100 or lower.

LIMIT UP, LIMIT DOWN-Commodity exchange restrictions on the maximum upward or downward movements permitted in the price for a commodity during any trading session day.

LINE, DOW THEORY-A Line in the Dow Theory is an Intermediate Sideways Movement in one or both of the Averages (Industrial and/or Transportation) in the course of which prices fluctuate within a range of 5% (of mean price) or less. (5% may be an outdated parameter.)

LIQUIDATION-At first meaning the sale or disposal of assets. Often used to indicate panic selling.

LOGARITHMIC SCALE-See Semilogarithmic Scale.

MAJOR TREND-In Edwards and Magee, the term Major (or Primary) refers to a trend (or pattern leading to such a trend) which lasts at least one year, and shows a rise or decline of at least 20% (a percentage probably outdated by modern markets).

MARGIN-The minimum amount of capital required to buy or sell a stock. The rate, currently 50% of value, is set by the government. In a commodity, margin is also the minimum, usually about 10%, needed to buy or sell a contract. But the rate is set by the individual exchanges. The two differ in cost as well. In a stock, the broker lends the investor the balance of the money due and charges interest for the loan. In a commodity, margin is treated as a good faith payment. The broker does not lend the difference, so no interest expense is incurred.

MARKET ON CLOSE-An order specification which requires the broker to get the best price available on the close of trading.

MARKET ORDER-An instruction to buy or sell at the price prevailing when the order reaches the floor of the exchange.

MAST-The vertical rally or reaction preceding a Flag or Pennant Formation.

MEASURING FORMULA-There are certain patterns which do allow the chartist the opportunity to project at least an interim target level of the direction of the Primary Trend. The most important of these patterns are found to be Triangles, Rectangles, Head-and-Shoulders, Pennants and Flags.

Triangles-When a stock breaks out of Symmetrical Triangle (either up or down), the ensuing move should carry at least as far as the height of the Triangle as measured along its first reaction.

Rectangles-The minimum you would expect from a breakout (up or down) out of a Rectangle Pattern would be the distance equal to the height of the formation.

Head-and-Shoulders Tops/Bottoms-The Head-and-Shoulders Pattern has one of the better measuring sticks. In either a Top or Bottom, the interim target, once the neckline is penetrated, is the distance from the Top (or Bottom) of the head to the level of the neckline directly below (above) the head.

Pennants and Flags-The one thing to remember about these Continuation Patterns is that they "fly at half-mast." In other words, the leg in equals the leg out.

MEASURING GAP-See Runaway Gap.

MEGAPHONES-Megaphones are Broadening Tops. The Broadening Formation may evolve in any one of the three forms comparable, respectively, to Inverted Symmetrical, Inverted Ascending or Descending Triangles. The symmetrical type, for example, consists of a series of price fluctuations across a horizontal axis, with each Minor Top higher and each Minor Bottom lower than its predecessor. The pattern may thus be roughly marked off by two diverging lines, the upper sloping up from left to right, the lower sloping down. These Broadening Patterns are characteristically loose and irregular, whereas Symmetrical Triangles are regular and compact. The converging boundary lines of Symmetrical Triangles are clearly defined, as a rule. Tops and Bottoms within the formation tend to fall within fair precision on these boundary lines. In the Broadening Formation, the rallies and declines usually do not all stop at clearly marked boundary lines and are subject to spikes. We could call this a Megaphone Spike because the formation keeps on crowding at the lines to look like a megaphone. It has a tendency to spike down more than up.

MINOR TREND-In Edwards and Magee, the term Minor refers to brief fluctuations (usually less than six days and rarely longer than three weeks) which, in total, make up the Intermediate Trend.

MOMENTUM INDICATOR-A market indicator which utilizes volume statistics for predicting the strength or weakness of a current market and any overbought or oversold conditions, and to distinguish turning points within the market.

MOVING AVERAGE-A mathematical technique to smooth data. It is called moving because the number of elements are fixed, but the time interval advances. Old data must be removed when new data is added, which causes the average to "move along" with the progression of the stock or commodity.

MULTIPLE HEAD-AND-SHOULDERS PATTERN-See Complex Head-and-Shoulders.

NARROW RANGE DAY-A trading day with a narrower price range relative to the previous day's price range.

NECKLINE-In a Head-and-Shoulders Pattern, it is the line drawn across the two reaction lows (in a Top), or two rally highs (in a Bottom), which occur before and after the head. This line must be broken by 3% to confirm the Reversal. In a Diamond Pattern, which is similar to a Head-and-Shoulders Pattern, the neckline is bent in the shape of a V or inverted V. (See also Diamond and Head-and-Shoulders.)

NEGATIVE DIVERGENCE-When two or more Averages, indexes or indicators fail to show confirming trends.

NEW HIGH-A concept of Magee's Basing Points Procedure. Occurs when price exceeds previous high by 3%. A constant in Magee, a parameter in Bassetti.

ORDER-See Limit Order, Market Order, and Stop Order.

OSCILLATOR-A form of momentum or rate-of-change indicator which is usually valued from +1 to -1 or from 0% to 100%.

OVERBOUGHT-Market prices that have risen too steeply and too quickly.

OVERSOLD-Market prices that have declined too steeply and too quickly.

OVERBOUGHT/OVERSOLD INDICATOR-An indicator that attempts to define when prices have moved too far and too quickly in either direction, and thus are liable to a reaction.

PANIC-The second stage of a Bear Market when buyers thin out and sellers become more urgent. The downward trend of prices suddenly accelerates into an almost vertical drop while volume rises to climactic proportions. (See also Bear Market.)

PANIC BOTTOM-See Selling Climax.

PATTERN-See Area Pattern.

PEAK-See Top.

PENETRATION-The breaking of a pattern boundary line, trendline or Support and Resistance Level.

PENNANT-A Pennant is a Flag with converging, rather than parallel, boundary lines. (See also Flag.)

PRAGMATIC PORTFOLIO THEORY-An alternative to Modern Portfolio Theory presented in Technical

Analysis of Stock Trends, 9th Edition.

PREMATURE BREAKOUT-A breakout of an Area Pattern, then a retreat back into the pattern. Eventually, the trend will break out again and proceed in the same direction. At the time they occur, false breakouts and premature breakouts are indistinguishable from each other, or a genuine breakout.

PRIMARY TREND-See Major Trend.

PROGRAM TRADING-Trades based on signals from various computer programs, usually entered directly from the trader's computer to the market's computer system.

PROGRESSIVE STOP-A stop order which follows the market up or down. (See also Stop.)

PROTECTIVE STOP-A stop order used to protect gains or limit losses in an existing position. (See also Stop.)

PULLBACK-Return of prices to the boundary line of the pattern after a breakout to the downside. Return after an upside breakout is called a Throwback.

RAIL AVERAGE-See Dow-Jones Transportation Average, which was originally called the Rail Average.

RALLY-An increase in price which retraces part of the previous price decline.

RALLY TOPS-A price level that finishes a short-term rally in an ongoing trend.

RANGE-The difference between the high and low during a specific time period.

REACTION-A decline in price which retraces part of the previous price advance.

RECTANGLE-A trading area which is bounded on the Top and the Bottom with horizontal, or near horizontal, lines. A Rectangle can be either a Reversal or Continuation Pattern depending on the direction of the breakout. Minimum Measuring Formula: Add the width (difference between Top and Bottom) of the Rectangle to the breakout point.

RESISTANCE LEVEL-A price level at which a sufficient supply of stock is forthcoming to stop, and possibly turn back for a time, an uptrend.

RETRACEMENT-A price movement in the opposite direction of the previous trend.

RETURN LINE-See Ascending or Descending Trend Channels.

REVERSAL GAP-A chart formation where the low of the last day is above the previous day's range, with the close above midrange and above the open.

REVERSAL PATTERN-An Area Pattern which breaks out in a direction opposite to the previous trend. (See also Ascending Triangle, Broadening Formation, Broadening Top, Descending Triangle, Diamond, Dormant Bottom, Double Bottom or Top, Triple Bottom or Top, Head-and-Shoulders, Rectangle, Rounding Bottom or Top, Saucer, Symmetrical Triangle and Rising or Falling Wedge.)

RIGHT-ANGLED BROADENING TRIANGLE-Area Pattern with one boundary line horizontal and the other at an angle which, when extended, will converge with the horizontal line at some point to the left of the pattern. Similar in shape to Ascending and Descending Triangles, except they are inverted and look like Flat-Topped or Bottomed Megaphones. Right-Angled Broadening Formations generally carry Bearish implications regardless of which side is flat. But any decisive breakout (3% or more) through the horizontal boundary line has the same forceful significance as does a breakout in an Ascending or Descending Triangle.

RISING WEDGE-An Area Pattern with two upward slanting, converging trendlines. Normally, it takes more than three weeks to complete, and volume will diminish as prices move toward the apex of the pattern. The anticipated direction of the breakout in a Rising Wedge is down. Minimum Measuring Formula: A retracement of all the ground gained within the wedge.

RISK-Commonly considered to be variability in returns of the invested instrument.

RISK CHARACTERISTICS- The pattern of behavior of the instrument under study. Wide ranges in price of a commodity is riskier than a savings account whose principal does not vary in value.

ROUNDING BOTTOM-An Area Pattern which pictures a gradual, progressive and fairly symmetrical change in the trend from down to up. Both the Price Pattern (along its lows) and the Volume Pattern show a concave shape often called a Bowl or Saucer. There is no minimum measuring formula associated with this Reversal Pattern.

ROUNDING TOP-An Area Pattern which pictures a gradual, progressive and fairly symmetrical change in the trend from up to down. The Price Pattern, along its highs, shows a convex shape sometime called an Inverted Bowl. The Volume Pattern is concave shaped (a bowl) as trading activity declines into the peak of the Price Pattern, and increases when prices begin to fall. There is no measuring formula associated with this Reversal Pattern.

RUNAWAY GAP-A relatively wide gap in prices which occurs in an advance or decline gathering momentum. Also called a "Measuring Gap," since it frequently occurs at just about the halfway point between the breakout which started the move and the Reversal Day which calls an end to it. Minimum Measuring Formula: Take the distance from the original breakout point to the start of the gap, and add it to the other side of the gap.

RUNNING MARKET-A market wherein prices are moving rapidly in one direction with very few or no price changes in the opposite direction.

SCALE IN-SCALE OUT-The practice of committing an investment in units, or parts, a bit at a time. Also liquidating the investment in units. Selling on scale up (or down), or scaling in (or out).

SCALPER-A trader who attempts to profit from very small very short term price moves.

SECONDARY TREND-See Intermediate Trend.

SELLING CLIMAX-A period of extraordinary volume which comes at the end of a rapid and comprehensive decline which exhausts the margin reserves of many speculators or patience of investors. Total volume turnover may exceed any single day's volume during the previous upswing as Panic Selling sweeps through the stock or commodity. Also called a Clean-Out Day, a Selling Climax reverses the technical conditions of the market. Although it is a form of a One-Day Reversal, it can take more than one day to complete.

SHARPE RATIO-Equals expected return minus the risk free interest rate divided by the standard deviation of returns.

SHAKEOUT-A corrective move large enough to "shake-out" nervous investors before the Primary Trend resumes.

SHORTINTEREST-Thenumberofsharesthathavebeen sold short and not yet repurchased. This information monthly by the New York Stock Exchange.

SHORT SALE-A transaction where the entry position is to sell a stock or commodity first and to repurchase it (hopefully at a lower price) at a later date. In the stock market, shares you do not own can be sold by borrowing shares from the broker, and replacing them when the offsetting repurchase takes place. In the commodity market, contracts are created when a buyer and seller get together through a floor broker. As a result, the procedure to sell in the commodity market is the same as it is to buy.

SHOULDER-See Head-and-Shoulders Patterns.

SLIPPAGE-Difference between price sought (e.g. a system stop) and price achieved in the market.

SMOOTHING-A mathematical approach that removes excess data variability while maintaining a correct appraisal of the underlying trend. Perhaps.

SPIKE-A sharp rise in price in a single day or two.

STOCHASTIC-Literally means random except in number driven technical analysis.

STOP-A contingency order which is placed above the current market price if it is to buy, or below the current market price if it is to sell. A stop order becomes a market order only when the stock or commodity moves up to the price of the buy stop, or down to the price of a sell stop. A stop can be used to enter a new position or exit an old position. (See also Protective or Progressive Stop.)

STOP LOSS-See Protective Stop.

SUPPLY LINE-See Resistance.

SUPPORT LEVEL-The price level at which a sufficient amount of demand is forthcoming to stop, and possibly turn higher for a time, a downtrend.

SYMMETRICAL TRIANGLE-Also called a Coil. Can be a Reversal or Continuation Pattern. A sideways congestion where each Minor Top fails to attain the height of the previous rally and each Minor Bottom stopping above the level of the previous low. The result is upper and lower boundary lines which converge, if extended, to a point on the right. The upper boundary line must slant down and the lower boundary line must slant up, or it would be a variety of Wedge. Volume tends to diminish during formation. Minimum Formula: Add the widest distance within the Triangle to its breakout point.

SYSTEMIC RISK-Beta.

TEST-A term used to describe the activity of a stock or commodity when it returns to, "tests", the validity of a previous trendline, or Support or Resistance Level.

THREE-DAY-AWAY RULE-An arbitrary time period used by Edwards and Magee in marking suspected Minor Tops or Bottoms.

THROWBACK-Return of prices to the boundary line of the pattern after a breakout to the upside. Return after a downside breakout is called a Pullback.

TOP-See Broadening Top, Descending Triangle, Double Top, Head-and-Shoulders Top, Triple Top and Rounding Top.

TREND-The direction prices are moving in the same direction, or the tendency or proclivity to move in a straight line. (See also Ascending, Descending and Horizontal Parallel Trend Channels, Convergent Trend, Divergent Trend, Intermediate Trend, Major Trend and Minor Trend.)

TREND CHANNEL-A parallel probable price range centered about the most likely price line.

TRENDLINE-If we actually apply a ruler to a number of charted price trends, we quickly discover the line which most often is really straight in an uptrend is a line connecting the lower extremes of the Minor Recessions within these lines. In other words, an advancing wave in the stock market is composed of a series of ripples, and the bottoms of each of these ripples tend to form on, or very close to, an upward slanting straight line. The tops of the ripples are usually less even; sometimes they also can be defined by a straight line, but more often, they vary slightly in amplitude, and so any line connecting their upper tips would be more or less crooked. On a descending price trend, the line most likely to be straight is the one that connects the tops of the Minor Rallies within it, while the Minor Bottoms may or may not fall along a straight edge. These two lines-the one that slants up along the successive wave bottoms within a broad up-move and the one that slants down across successive wave tops within a broad downmove-are the Basic Trendlines. You draw an Up Trendline by drawing the line on the inner side. You draw a Down Trendline by drawing it on the outside. You draw a Sideways Trendline on the bottom.

TREND RISK-The risk intendant in being long a falling market without a stop. Modern Portfolio Theory inadequately accounts for this market fact. Fund managers accept it blithely.

TRIANGLE-See Ascending Triangle, Descending Triangle, Right-Angled Broadening Triangle, and Symmetrical Triangle.

TRIPLE BOTTOM-Similar to a flat Head-and-Shoulders Bottom, or Rectangle, the three Bottoms in a Triple Bottom.

TRIPLE TOP-An Area Pattern with three Tops which are widely spaced and with quite deep, and usually rounding, reactions between them. Less volume occurs on the second peak than the first peak, and still less on the third peak. Sometimes called a "W" Pattern, particularly if the second peak is below the first and third. The Triple Top is confirmed when the decline from the third Top penetrates the Bottom of the lowest valley between the three peaks.

200-DAY MOVING AVERAGE LINE-Is determined by taking the closing price over the past 200 trading days and dividing by 200.

UPTREND-See Ascending Trendline and Trend.

UTILITY AVERAGE-See Dow- Jones Utility Average.

VOLATILITY-A measure of a stock's tendency to move up and down in price, based on its daily price history over the latest 12 month period. Calculation of volatility is often reduced to the standard deviation.

WAVE HIGH-WAVE LOW-Extreme of a price wave, usually marked as a high day (or low) which is confirmed by the occurrence of three days of price activity outside the range of the high (low) day.

WEDGE-A chart formation in which the price fluctuations are confined within converging straight (or practically straight) lines.

WYCKOFF'S COMPOSITE OPERATOR-Wyckoff was a prominent early 20th century stock trader who was a keen observer of and theoretician of the market. Among his concepts is that of the "composite operator", by which he meant the combined forces of the market moving it up or down according to some inchoate (or perhaps choate) plan.

Bibliography

Belveal, L. Dee, *Charting Commodity Market Price Behavior,* 2nd ed., Dow Jones-Irwin, Homewood, IL, 1985.

Bernstein, Peter, *Against the Gods,* John Wiley & Sons, New York, 1996.

Bolton, A. Hamilton, *The Elliott Wave Principle. A Critical Appraisal,* Monetary Research, Hamilton, Bermuda, 1960,

Dunn & Hargitt *Trader's Notebook. Trading Methods Checked by Computer,* Dunn & Hargitt, Lafayette, IN, 1970.

Edwards, Robert D., Magee, John, Bassetti, W.H.C., *Technical Analysis of Stock Trends, 9th Ed., CRC Press, Boca Raton FL, 2007*

Elliott, Ralph N., *The Major Works of R.N. Elliott,* Prechter, R., Ed., New Classics Library, Chappaqua, NY, 1980.

Frost, Alfred J. and Robert R. Prechter, *Elliott Wave Principle, Key to Stock Market Profits,* New Classics Library, Chappaqua, NY, 1978.

Galbraith, John K., *The Great Crash 1929,* Houghton Mifflin, Boston, 1961.

Hamilton, William Peter, *The Stock Market Barometer,* John Wiley & Sons, New York, 1998 (1922)

Jiler, William L., *How Charts Can Help You in the Stock Market,* Trendline, New York, 1962.

Jorion, Philippe, *Value at Risk,* John Wiley & Sons, New York, 1996.

Kaufman, Perry J., *Commodity Trading Systems and Methods,* Wiley, New York, 1978.

Kaufman, Perry J., *Technical Analysis in Commodities,* John Wiley & Sons, New York, 1980.

MacKay, Charles, *Extraordinary Popular Delusions and the Madness of Crowds,* Three Rivers Press, New York, 1980.

Magee, John, *Analyzing Bar Charts for Profit,* John Magee Inc. (now St. Lucie Press, Boca Raton FL), 1994.

Magee, John, *Winning the Mental Game on Wall Street,* (2nd edition of *The General Semantics of Wall Street*), edited by W.H.C. Bassetti, St. Lucie Press, Boca Raton, FL, 2000.

Mandelbrot, B.., "A MultiFractal Walk Down Wall Street," *Scientific American,* February 1999, June 1999.

Niederhoffer, Victor, *The Education of a Speculator,* John Wiley & Sons, New York, 1997.

Nison, Steve, *Beyond Candlesticks,* John Wiley & Sons, New York, 1994.

Nison, Steve, *Japanese Candlestick Charting Techniques,* New York Institute of Finance, New York, 1991.

O'Neil, William J., *How to Make Money in Stocks,* 2nd ed., McGraw-Hill, New York, 1995.

Schultz, John W., *The Intelligent Chartist,* WRSM Financial Services, New York, 1962.

Schwager, Jack, *Schwager on Futures, Technical Analysis,* John Wiley & Sons, New York, 1996.

Schwager, Jack D., *Market Wizards,* Harper Business, New York, 1990.

Schwager, Jack D., *The New Market Wizards,* Harper Business, New York, 1992.

Shibayama, Zebkei, *Zen Comments on the Mumonkan,* Harper and Row, New York, 1974.

Sklarew, Arthur, *Techniques of a Professional Commodity Chart Analyst,* Commodity Research

Bureau, New York, 1980.

Teweles, Richard J., Charles V. Harlow, and Herbert L. Stone, *The Commodity Futures Game — Who Wins? — Who loses? — Why?,* 2nd ed., McGraw-Hill, New York, 1974.

Vodopich, Donald R., *Trading For Profit With Precision Timing,* Precision Timing, Atlanta, GA, 1984.

Wheelan, Alexander H., *Study Helps in Point and Figure Technique,* Morgan Rogers, 1966.

Wilder, J. Welles, *New Concepts in Technical Trading Systems,* Trend Research, Greensboro, NC, 1978.

Williams, Larry R., *How I Made $1,000,000 Trading Commodities Last Year,* 3rd ed., Conceptual Management, Monterey, CA, 1979.

Zweig, Martin, *Winning on Wall Street,* Warner Books, New York, 1986.

FURTHER STUDY: The edwards-magee.com website.

For about thirty years – from the fifties to the eighties – John Magee wrote a weekly investment letter. It was mailed out every Friday –a collection of handsome charts and commentary which was notable for its pragmatism and wisdom.

Since 1999 W.H.C. Bassetti has published on the web a letter comparable to that published by Magee. At least once a week and usually two or three times he comments on the market.

One of the readers recently commented that the edwards-magee letter is the most useful investment letter he has taken since he used to take Magee's service.

As an example of the effectiveness of the letter – it has been long the gold market since 2003. It exited the market in January 2008 at 12603 and shorted and remained short through the writing of this note in March 2009.

A subscription to the letter comes with a number of premiums – books and ebooks.

To subscribe go to edwards-magee.com

The past performance of the letter may be examined in detail for 2007 and 2008 with these addresses:
www.edwards-magee.com/nf07/0700.html
www.edwards-magee.com/nf08/0800.html

INFORMATION ON OTHER BOOKS AND WEB LETTER

Technical Analysis of Stock Trends is free with a subscription to the edwards-magee.com website.

Now in its 9th edition with about 1,000,000 copies in print Technical Analysis of Stock Trends by Edwards and Magee as revised and modernized by W.H.C. Bassetti. It is the definitive textbook and manual on the practice of technical analysis through the analysis of charts. It is probably accurate to say that all technical analysis has its roots in this book. And it is also true that the provenance of this book boasts a lineage of masters of the craft which goes back to Charles Dow.

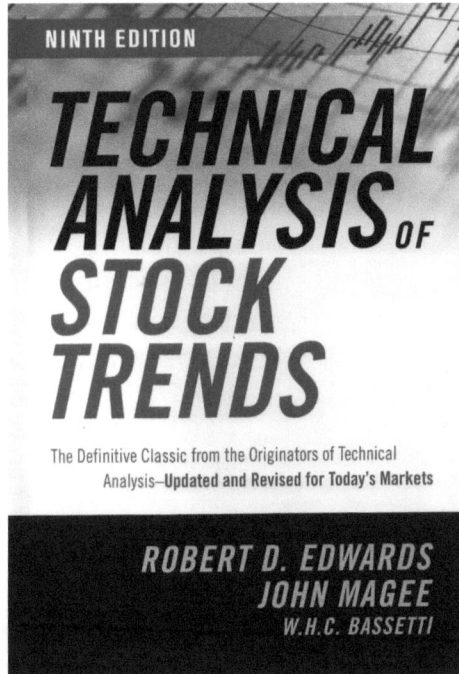

Dow begat Hamilton who begat Schabacker who begat Edwards who partnered with John Magee to produce the first edition in 1948 after a long and laborious process of reviewing Schabacker's and Dow's work. Edwards left the partnership before Bassetti knew Magee. So Magee produced alone the then definitive 4th and 5th editions. Magee sold his company to Richard McDermott who produced the 6th and 7th Editions. Virtually all of the editions were reprinted many times, as, from the first edition, investors immediately recognized the value of the work.

This 9th edition is coauthored by W.H.C. Bassetti of john magee technical analysis::delphic options research ltd. The 9th Edition maintains the integrity of the original and updates those areas which need to be updated. It leaves untouched vast parts of the book which are as pertinent today as when they were first created by Edwards and Magee. Added to the 9th Edition were materials on risk and portfolio analysis as well as extensive material on technological and finance developments.

Many imitations of this book exist. In general they are not so incisive and not so well written. And sad to say, usually dry and boring. After reading the book the alert reader will see its material reproduced in book after book. In fact this is the only book the trader/investor needs on this subject. There is nothing new that can be said about technical analysis of stock trends through chart analysis.

Much praise has been lavished on the book:

"This book is a classic--the standard of excellence against which everything in technical analysis is measured. I am delighted to know that another generation of investors will be able to learn from this wonderful book."

Ralph Acampora, Director of Technical Research, Prudential Securities

"The #1 all-time classic on analysis of bar charts. Many knowledgeable technicians consider this to be the best book on chart patterns ever written! It is an absolute MUST for any student of technical analysis." Edward Dobson, President, Traders Press, Inc.

"There is no better place to begin your education in market behavior than this pioneering book. It has stood the test of time and will continue to apply in the future, because the engine of market patterns and human social psychology never changes."

Robert Prechter, Elliott Wave International

The fact that this text is still being reprinted 53 years after its initial publication should tell you all you need to know. It is as relevant to today's markets as ever. The companies may have changed, but the patterns haven't. This edition contains the basics of trading stock indexes, discussions on options, risk, the significance of technology on technical analysis and trading and numerous other additions. In short, it remains an essential volume for students and practitioners of chart analysis.

Jack Schwager, author of Market Wizards

"Completely revised and updated, this highly acclaimed book teaches us how to profit from chart patterns regardless of what the market is doing. This classic book on chart patterns is a must for the savvy trader. Investors employing the trading techniques outlined in this updated edition when buying or selling a stock will achieve superior results." David Robinson, Publisher, The Bull & Bear Financial Report.

Sacred Chickens, the Holy Grail and Dow Theory

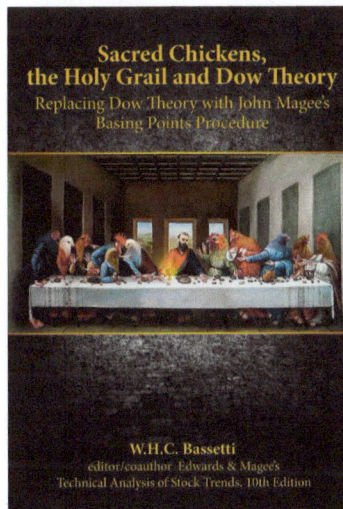

This book examines the performance of Dow Theory from its beginning to the end of 2007. It compares this performance with the results of trading signals from the Magee Basing Points Procedure.

The Dow Theory as enunciated by Charles Dow and William Peter Hamilton is the grandfather of all technical analysis. As it grew, like Topsy, it has its eccentricities and its anomalies. But over the time of its observation, from 1897 to the present it has compiled an impressive performance record for those who had the foresight to take its signals. As it has a number of conditions and rules which must occur to create a buy or sell signal Charles Bassetti jokingly compared it to the ancient Roman practice of divining the future by examining the entrails of chickens. Jokes aside the Theory is a serious method for dealing with long term investments in the market.

John Magee's Basing Point Procedure, as further articulated by Bassetti, is run on all the Dow Industrial data to determine how, as a system, it would compare with the results of Dow Theory. The results are enlightening and the process of studying the interaction of the two methods and what they do in the market is an invaluable exercise for one who would be a long term investor.

In fact and this can be emphasized neither method has ever left the long term investor long the market in a prolonged bear market as has occurred from 2008-2009. Let us repeat that. Both methods sold long market positions before the crucial damage was done.

Introduction to the Magee System of Technical Analysis

Now in its 9th edition with about 1,000,000 copies in print Technical Analysis of Stock Trends by Edwards and Magee as revised and modernized by W.H.C. Bassetti. It is the definitive textbook and manual on the practice of technical analysis through the analysis of charts. It is probably accurate to say that all technical analysis has its roots in this book. And it is also true that the provenance of this book boasts a lineage of masters of the craft which goes back to Charles Dow.

The ideal approach to Technical Analysis of Stock Trends is this present book, written and revised especially for that purpose from its first edition by Magee, by W.H.C. Bassetti. The 9th Edition is rich, complex and subtle--and very long. The Introduction gives a newcomer a concise conceptual grasp of the content of the 9th. It allows him to practice without further study, or to proceed to more advanced study in the 9th from a firm intellectual foundation.

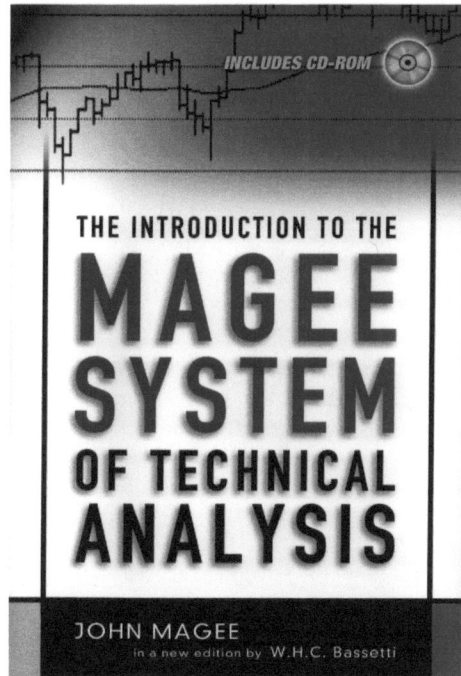

This edition is much praised by professionals in the field.

Professor Henry Pruden, a world authority on technical analysis made these remarks in his review of the book: "John Magee's Analyzing Bar Charts for Profit was, in its first edition, one of the better introductions to technical analysis for the beginner. Now in its second edition with modernizations and annotations by Charles Bassetti, it is the best introduction to the craft of chart analysis. Adding to the elegant presentation of Magee, the master, Bassetti, his student, has admirably rounded out the book with illustrations and examples from other areas of technical analysis as well as providing a vital summation of the Magee Method. This is one of the best books with which to begin the study of technical analysis."

Mark Wainwright of Paradigm Trading Systems, successor to the distinguished firm, Options Research Inc, assayed the book as follows: "Just as Technical Analysis of Stock Trends (8th Ed.) is the definitive work on chart analysis, this book is the definitive introduction to technical analysis. Books on technical analysis are often stiff, overly mathematical and boring. This book is a welcome exception. It is concise, interesting and well written, in short an excellent beginning for beginners.

Winning the Mental Game on Wall Street

Now in its 9th edition with about 1,000,000 copies in print Technical Analysis of Stock Trends by Edwards and Magee as revised and modernized by W.H.C. Bassetti. It is the definitive textbook and manual on the practice of technical analysis through the analysis of charts. It is probably accurate to say that all technical analysis has its roots in this book. And it is also true that the provenance of this book boasts a lineage of masters of the craft which goes back to Charles Dow.

The ideal philosophical and psychological approach to Technical Analysis of Stock Trends is this present book, (originally titled (The General Semantics of Wall Street). It has been rewritten and revised especially for the purpose of dealing with the mental aspects of investing by W.H.C. Bassetti.

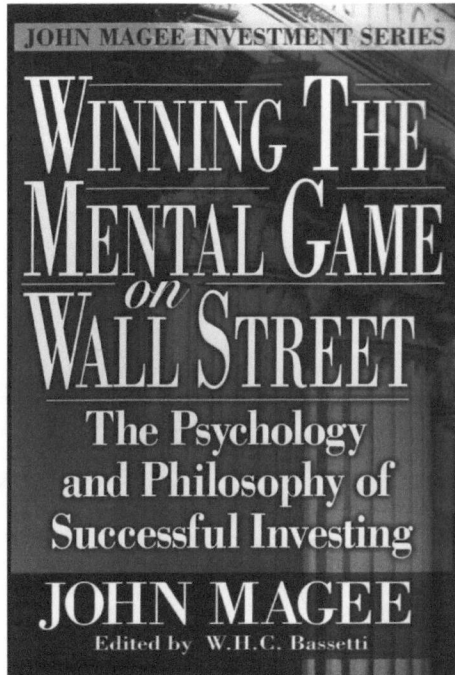

JOHN MAGEE INVESTMENT SERIES

WINNING THE MENTAL GAME on WALL STREET

The Psychology and Philosophy of Successful Investing

JOHN MAGEE
Edited by W.H.C. Bassetti

The 9th Edition is rich, complex and subtle. But it does not deal directly with the philosophy and psychology of trading. For many years Magee taught a course called The General Semantics of Wall Street (title of the first edition of this book). Effectively the course, and this book reprogram the reader's mind to permit effective and mentally unencumbered thinking about investing and trading.

This edition is much praised by professionals in the field.

Mark Wainwright, President of Paradigm Trading Systems, an authority on technical analysis, made these remarks in his review of the book: "John Magee's General Semantics of Wall Street, now titled Winning the Mental Game on Wall Street, is startlingly effective in making the reader think about the way he thinks about the markets and trading. No investor should be without it."

10 Trading Lessons (Bottoms) Available at edwards-magee.com

In a bear market it's a good idea to know what bear market bottoms look like. This book illustrates the classical patterns as identified by Edwards and Magee, and studies their application in the great Bush Bear of 2008-2009. Other markets and time periods are also illustrated.

Replete with examples it takes not only theoretical material but also live charts from the Bush Bear to give the reader the unusual perspective of real time analysis and subsequent consideration in tranquility.

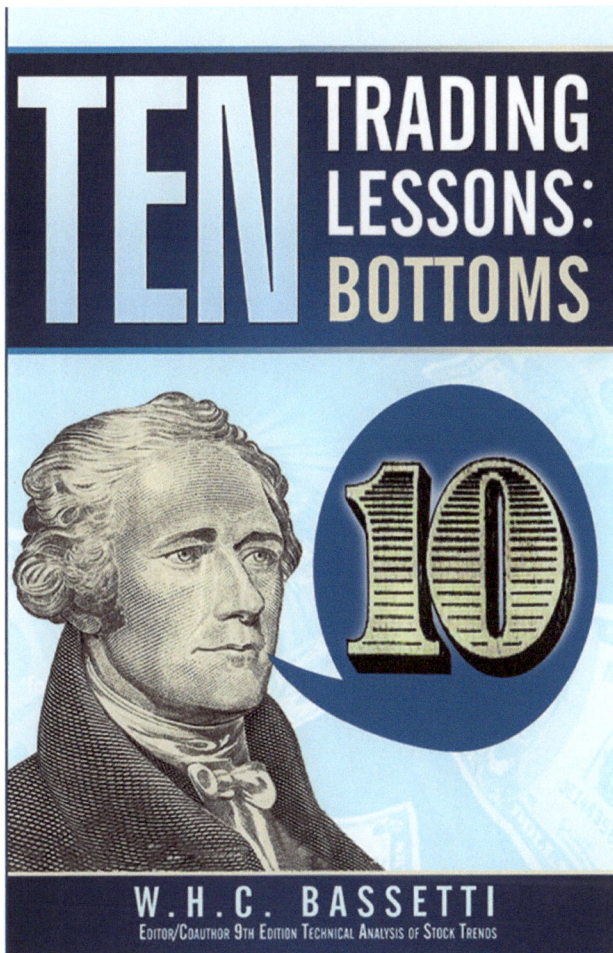

TEN TRADING LESSONS: BOTTOMS

10

W.H.C. BASSETTI

Editor/Coauthor 9th Edition Technical Analysis of Stock Trends

The Glon Charts

Quite possibly the most interesting charts ever made of the Dow Industrials, Chris Glon's charts record all of the signals from Dow Theory and from the Magee Basing Point Procedure and display it in charts of almost infinitely variable size – up to wall size.

Posting trade signals on the chart with their associated data allows the student to experience directly the effectiveness of the methods and see where the systems are extraordinarily skillful in the market and where the market defeats them (not in many places).

Zen Simple Beat the Market with a Ruler

This unusual book is an ideal starting point for an investor new to the market, or new to managing his own investments. With the discrediting of the mutual fund industry in the great bear market of 2008-09 many investors are turning to investing in ETFs, and this book shows the investor with exquisite simplicity how to manage those trades and investments. That is the point of the ruler of the title.

The methods are so simple that anyone with a high school education – or the self taught who can read, add and multiply – can manage stock trades better than many professionals.

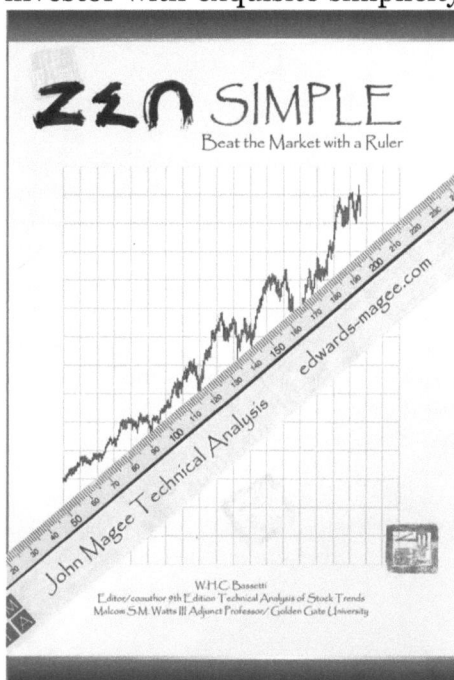

While the book is ideal for these investors it would also be good reading for mutual fund managers and hedge fund managers. A hysterically funny fact of the great bear market is that Morningstar gave its Manager of the Year Award for 2008 to a mutual fund manager who lost 16.9%. (Because all the other mutual funds did enormously worse.) While most of these people were losing 47% or more in the great bear market the author of this book sold the market short in January of 2008 and was short through the entire fall. This prescient transaction was accomplished using the methods described in this book.

"This deceptively simple little book is an ideal

introduction to chart analysis for the investor or trader who has never looked into it, or for a newcomer to the market. The method itself is amazingly powerful and amazingly simple, as evidenced by the author's having shorted the market in January 2008 long before mutual fund managers and other "professionals" were even aware of the looming danger of the subprime mortgage crisis.

Mark L. Wainwright
President, Paradigm Trading Systems.

Technical Analysis of Stock Trends
The 2 ¹/² day Seminar

Comments by some past students

This course was an outstanding course. It clarified and expanded my understanding of trends. I was further enlightened as to the flaws of (my) trading style. Charles Bassetti is the Socrates of technical analysis, or certainly one of the greatest teachers I have ever had. I hope to learn more from him.

Experience: A++

This was an excellent experience for me. I haven't traded actively in several years and it's been 3+ years since I was last involved in learning TA. I was amazed at the simplicity of the techniques discussed and the fact that they can be applied mid and long-term without the need to sit in front of the computer everyday actively monitoring the markets. Doing this during my previous experience was a turnoff, especially since I was learning on the fly and didn't have a solid understanding of one or more basic theories, which I was able to gain in this seminar. I am now confident I will be able to take this new knowledge and put it to immediate use. Thanks.

I feel Charles Bassetti's 2 $^{1/2}$ day seminar was both practical and insightful. I am excited to put into practice all that I learned. I am confident my future trading experiences will be profitable using the information I have learned. I would recommend this seminar to anyone experienced or otherwise who is serious about their trading.

Instructor's Report Card:

I really enjoyed the class. The quality of instruction & format were excellent. I'm looking forward to using the trading concepts.

Excellent Overview of subject. Plus I enjoyed it.

Grade E= Excellent Will give you a report after it all sinks in.

ENLIGHTENED:

This class has helped me bring my trading back to reality... seeing stocks for what they are.

See the flower: This stuff really works-- it is not what I had previously heard it to be --

Grade AAA+:

This course is excellent. Particularly because in the first day you managed to simplify and anchor the basis of charting. Your approach to charting is pure and objective. This is significant for me because previously I looked at the chart seeking a pattern, however if I just get out the ruler and draw --then my analysis can tell me, just as you say. That is a seriously critical point. Thank you.

Course grade A: I enjoyed it and learned a great deal. The exercises were important and valuable. Thanks!

Please spend more time on forms of hedging and forms of arbitrage. Also, this workshop/seminar has been an excellent review of trading principles.

Scans of the handwritten report cards from which these comments were taken may be seen at edwards-magee. com/NewFiles/grades.html.

On Mar 8, 2007, at 10:57 AM, <tony.c@oocl.com>
<tony.c@oocl.com> wrote:

Prof. Bassetti,

I'm a former student of your's at GGU – technical
analysis class. I resisted technical analysis for a long time
as I was too focused on fundamentals and valuation.
In fact, what you taught me some 5 years ago has finally
sunk in. I now use fundamentals for stock screening,
but use technical analysis for entries and exits.

Anyway, just want to say thanks. I should have listen to
you a long time ago.

Best Regards,

Tony C.

Orient Overseas Container Line

All I ever needed to know about buying and selling
stock I learned from Charles Bassetti. I have used just
two foundation techniques that I learned in Charles'
class, those of basing points and trendlines over the
last two years and have not had a loosing trade since!
And that's just the beginning of what he has to
offer......

THANK YOU CHARLES!!!!

Brenda S.

Professor,

As I sat sipping coffee and watching the Treasury
Secretary gasping for air to speak this morning - looking
to me like a mouse in a darkened room caught by the
lights being turned on (don't know the man, nothing

personal - just an observation), I took comfort that my pulse rate was low and my evaluation of the markets buffered by a chart.

Thanks for leading me on my journey - I have so far to go. (As I guess we all do until we go no further, eh?).

But, had I not had the experiences of 498, and the lessons of Magee in those two wonderful books, along the way, I would be a basket case today - and likely for the months preceding and following.

I can really appreciate the calm that the charts assist me with my psyche.

All the best from an admiring student...

Alan B.

www.ingramcontent.com/pod-product-compliance
Lightning Source LLC
Chambersburg PA
CBHW041446210326
41599CB00004B/147